Mexico Got Lucky

Rico Austin, PhD

Briley & Baxter Publications | Plymouth, Massachusetts

ISBN: 978-1-954819-39-9

Book & cover design by Amy Deyerle-Smith
Edited by Eleonor Gardner

I would like to dedicate this 2nd edition of *Mexico Got Lucky* to my great friend, the late Mr. Jim Kawaguchi, who never gave up looking for his stolen, fur baby–LUCKY!!!

Jim Kawaguchi, RIP
Born: 7-22-1961
Eternal rest: 2-27-2017

I wish to dedicate *A New Beginning for Dogs* to Barb of Barb's Pet Rescue and to pet lovers the world over, for those who care for and work endlessly to help provide food and shelter for abandoned and unwanted pets. Also, I wish to dedicate this to those non-profit organizations and clubs who help promote the spaying/neutering of pets to eliminate more unwanted animals onto this globe.

New photos supplied by Jim's loving wife, Lourdes Paz Kawaguchi

Jim with his father-in-law Raul enjoying a meal

Jim and Raul

Jim and Raul at San Carlos fishing dock with their catch of yel-

Jim and his wife, Lourdes, enjoying a day on the water

Jim on a ladder thinking about his next move

Jim and Lourdes with Lourdes's parents during Oktoberfest

Jim and Lourdes

Jim and Lourdes

Lucky proud of his new haircut

Lucky and a buddy

Table of Contents

Part 1: Mexico Got Lucky

 # Preface

While writing *Mexico Got Lucky*, I heard many different dog stories from other caring pet parents, and visited dog pounds and rescue centers, and felt that I had to share some of what I learned, and write of the great organizations and people in Mexico that are trying their best to find homes for these abandoned, helpless pets.

This book contains short stories, some quotes, and places of caring where a person might adopt a dog in Mexico. It is a collection of writings, that show the greatness of the human heart and sacrifices made by many of these volunteers on a daily basis. Some of the following chapters are of what I've found on the internet, some of them I've witnessed, and some of them are from inside me.

Acknowledgments

I wish to thank Jim Kawaguchi for sharing with me parts of his private life so that I might write his story with justice and truth.

I wish to thank all of those who commented on the Lucky blog and those that checked in for the daily and weekly updates that were posted to the blog via the www.VivaSanCarlos.mx bulletin board to stay updated on the fate of Lucky, the most famous dog in Sonora, Mexico. Over 25,000 blog views mentioning "Lucky" and his disappearance made this the most popular "Topic/Subject" in the history of www.VivaSanCarlos.mx, by a landslide.

Thanks to the entire communities of San Carlos, Guaymas, Hermosillo, Empalme and Obregón for joining in the search.

A warm wish and thank you to the musicians, restaurant and bar owners, and to the volunteers of San Carlos and Guaymas, who dedicated their music performances, their establishments, food and drink, and their time with superb effort to promote charities for children and animals of the neighboring communities. I am indeed, truly "Lucky" to live and breathe among you in the most beautiful part of the world.

A special thank you to my wife Connie, for pushing me to reach just a little deeper within my writing soul to make each story capture the hearts of my readers. I also wish to thank her for designing the front and back covers of all my books; she gets it right, each and every time.

A special tribute goes out to my editor, Miss Bonnie Lee who passed away unexpectedly on July 7, 2015, before I could send the manuscript of this story to her to receive her always positive and welcomed feedback. Bonnie, you will be missed by many within the literary world and the wine world, both of which you loved dearly and were loved by. RIP.

¡Viva MEXICO!

1 🐾 Just Another
Day in Paradise

February 28th, 2014

Latitude: 27.58 degrees North
Longitude: 111.06 degrees West

As I lounge lazily in a white plastic chair with a Mexican beer logo scrawled in red across the back, I watch as a fishing boat about twenty-four to twenty-six feet long glides smoothly into shallow water along the coast of the Sea of Cortez. At almost the same instant, a tanned gringo approximately fifty years of age heaves an anchor into about fifteen feet of water, three ladies and another man toss themselves into the sea and begin swimming or dog paddling the twenty yards or so to the beach.

I'm chillaxin' at the beachside Soggy Peso, AKA The Hangout, situated on the fairest stretch of white beach in the Mexican state of Sonora.

A couple of miles northwest of San Carlos lie the soft, white, powdery sand of Algodones Playa (Cotton Beach), which is home to Playa Blanca Condos that rise fifteen stories into the blue sky, the five-storied San Carlos Plaza Hotel Resort, and less than half a dozen beach bars. The former Club Med, now known as Paradiso Resort Beach Club, and Playa Blanca act as borders to the Soggy Peso, La Salsa, Bonifacio's Cotton Club, and possibly another one or two of which their names escape me. Bonifacio's main building has been refurbished, redecorated, and renovated from its former self as The Night Club, owned by and on the property of Club Mediterranean, a French-owned corporation with vacation resorts found in many parts of the world, usually in exotic locations. These libation huts and palapas are so closely built to each other it is oftentimes difficult to know where one property ends and another begins.

The reason I sit and waste away another beautiful day in paradise at Soggy Peso is because of loyalty; it was the first place established with música and a refreshing cold drink this far from the small, but growing, tourist town. One half of my wooden table stands drenching in the sun, the other half is cooled by the shade of the heavily thatched, woven, Mexican palm fronds. La Salsa and Bonifacio's Cotton Club are both great beachside watering holes with service that keeps a guy and gal returning. At those places and here is where you'll find the surfer-looking dudes and dudettes that steal away from Arizona State or the University of Arizona for a three-day holiday break; fishermen of all sorts–weekend deep-sea anglers, Alaskan crabbers enjoying the offseason, and those that depend on a good day's catch nearly every day to pay the rent and afford the occasional cerveza alongside the tourists.

As I scan the crowd, I'm sure there might be a felon or two; an overworked doctor; an overpaid attorney; a stressed-out educator; a lounging construction worker; a writer enjoying a tasty margarita laced with his favorite tequila and time spent away from the computer while banging away another story in his head; a waitress who has been waiting for this deserving day for over six months, finally able to be on the receiving side of service with a smile; and perhaps another entrepreneur like myself, just wanting to see and listen to the sea wash gently, wave upon wave, to the shore.

The party of four who abandoned the boat is now out of the water and walk towards me and the bar. The captain of the boat, a middle-aged man that dropped the anchor off the boat, has now jumped into the cool, early spring waters of the Cortez, soon to join his amigos.

My attention is drawn to the west as the sun begins to settle on the ocean, dancing with sparkles of light jolting from the slight ripples of the calm sea. In just a matter of seconds, I take a snapshot with my phone before it is lost, only to be found in the eastern skies in the form of a sunrise.

The slender musician wearing Levi's, a long-sleeve shirt rolled up to the forearm, and standing in flip flops, picks up his guitar in front of the primitive stage made up of a slab of concrete and bamboo poles tied together with strands of strong, weedy grass standing vertically as a backdrop. "Hey, how about that sunset behind me! I'm Eric and... ."

I look at my curly, white buddy enjoying his late afternoon nap, lounging in the shadow of the table with the soft sand beneath his body. I glance over at the mural painted on the wall that reads, "Latitude 27.58 Degrees North, Longitude 111.06 Degrees West," and I smile.

Buenas noches,
Jim

2 🐾 Estuary – not a Haven for Dogs

What would you do if someone you dearly loved was unexpectedly taken from you?

To what lengths would you enter? How far would you go to get a member of your family back?

I had never thought about these questions, and many others like it before Lucky went missing. It was the first time in my life that a loved one of mine had been taken, and little did I know that I would be tested to the brink of sanity and poor health, resulting from an existing chronic health condition; this would become a factor in possibly never seeing my Lucky Boy, again.

"No dogs allowed at the estuary," I did not think another thing about it. This was not an extraordinary request, as there were several times in the past where man's best friend, dogs, were not allowed in a certain area or place.

The unfortunate "incident" began on Saturday, March 1st. It was the beginning of a beautiful, glorious day with Lucky and I talking to each other. I said, "I Love You" to him a couple of times, and he responded by howling back "I Love You." We had been invited to take a cruise along the bahía (bay) with friends. Letty and I had brought wine, beer, and food as we were going to make a half-day of it including lunch à la picnic style. After a relaxing, fun jaunt around the mountains and rocks that protected the bay from the Sea of Cortez, we brought the boat back into the marina and loaded the car

up as we still had plenty of food and alcohol to take back to the
house for later.

I believe it was around 5:00 p.m., the winter sun was not high in the Mexican sky, when Letty, a good friend of mine, suggested that we visit the estuary right next to Pilar Condos since there was still plenty of daylight remaining of this fun Saturday. Letty, Lucky, and I had just left the marina after spending a couple of fun hours cruising around the San Carlos Marina with Philip—a good friend and neighbor—on his boat.

I had not been introduced to this protected area called the "estuario" that is part of the equation that helps make up San Carlos. The establishment of Pilar Condos was built next to the estuary just southeast of San Carlos about two miles from town. Pilar was made famous by Burl Ives, who stood against the Mexican Military and demanded that all condos be reinstated to their rightful owners back in the 1960s. Burl Ives is and was a hero to all those that have property at Pillar, or anywhere in Mexico, and to those that have or had a dream of purchasing property in Mexico.

Being one to follow rules, I did not argue with Letty's instructions: Lucky would stay in the car since the temperature was below seventy degrees Fahrenheit that cool afternoon. I let the windows down, about five inches, and the sunroof was open to allow Lucky to have plenty of air and scents of the sea.

The estuary or *Estero el Soldado*, the correct given name in Spanish, is a mangrove-lined estuary that connects freshwater with that of the Sea of Cortez. It was my first time visiting the tranquil setting with a nice trail from the area in which people parked their cars on the edge of the sand. It was not a formal parking lot, just sand with lots of tracks from different vehicles of mostly local and vacationing Mexicans out to enjoy Mother Nature and the scenery.

Letty, the hostess that she is, was pointing out the crabs and minnows while introducing me to the new surroundings and telling me about the estuary when the alarm of my Mercedes Benz went screaming into alert mode. Within minutes I hustled back to my four-door sedan just 150-200 yards away to find no Lucky! Frantically I looked about the area and called out to him, hoping that Lucky would come running into my arms. No Lucky! *What the heck!* I thought. And the losers had not only taken our wine, our food—they took my son! The hurt in my heart from finding that Lucky was missing was nothing compared to the anger at whoever took "my boy." My thoughts spiraled: *I will catch the thief and tie him or her to the highest level of impurity. You lowlifes know who you are and guess what? A little time will not garner what you believe it to be, because we will hunt you down and...May GOD have mercy upon your souls, because I will not.*

My name is Jim. I'm not "purebred" and neither is my "mutt" Lucky, a reference I affectionately gave to him. Lucky is the only member of my family that lives with me. Kawaguchi is my family's last name. It was given to me by a Japanese man that not only adopted me, but gave me a name that is well respected and revered in many parts of the globe.

I was born a child without a father and to a mother that had believed a man of Grecian heritage named Constantine would marry her. She was an innocent, naïve, young woman who'd mistaken lies from an adulterer, for love. The man that laid with my mother could not leave his wife, but easily left my mother an unmarried, pregnant, young waitress working at Stouffers Restaurant in Cleveland, Ohio.

Two years later, my Polish mother met a great human being named, "David Koji Kawaguchi" who had spent time behind prison fences in Gila Bend, Arizona during World War II. The only reason my adopted dad was sent to Gila Bend to be caged like an animal was because of his Japanese heritage, even though he was an American citizen and loved the United States completely with his heart. This epic travesty happened for many Japanese American citizens during World War II, where because of their ethnicity, were sent to "War Relocation Camps."

The internment of Japanese Americans was authorized with Executive Order 9066 by then-President Franklin D. Roosevelt on February 19th, 1942, that allowed local military commanders to designate "military areas" as "exclusion zones." The U.S. government ordered the internment shortly after Imperial Japan's attack on Pearl Harbor the morning of December 7th, 1941 bringing the United States into the Second World War. This executive power was used to exclude all people of Japanese ancestry from the entire Pacific coast, even if the internees were American citizens. The U.S. Census Bureau played a substantial role in the internment efforts by forwarding confidential neighborhood information on Japanese Americans of which it continually denied for decades. In 2007, it was finally proven that the Census Bureau was indeed involved in providing information.

President Ronald Reagan signed into law the Civil Liberties Act in 1988 that apologized for the internment of Japanese Americans on behalf of the U.S. government, and authorized a payment of $20,000 to each individual camp survivor. My dad received his check. The legislation admitted that government actions were based on "war hysteria, race prejudice, and failed political leadership." More than $1.6 billion in atonement money was dispersed among 82,219 Japanese families and/or their heirs.[1]

My dad shared many stories with me about his time spent confined. He was only ten years old when first detained. As I think back on this whole experience with Lucky, it has really made me think long and hard about what my father, his parents, and thousands of others went through, being caged like unwanted animals.

Why is this so important to me and the story? Just as unwanted dogs are placed in inhumane, small, and unclean kennels, so were the Americans of Japanese descent put behind barbed wire encampments losing their freedom to pursue happiness. In the Declaration of Independence, the pursuit of happiness is defined as the fundamental right to freely pursue joy and live life in a way that makes you happy (as long as you don't do anything illegal or violate the rights of others). Both dogs and the American Japanese have been caged for no other reason than being born into their own unique circumstances.

During my long, endless search for Lucky, I witnessed so many dogs in small kennels. These caged, undernourished, dehydrated, and unloved dogs have been sentenced to death at no fault or wrongdoing of their own. They have been born in a society where a dog with no pedigree has little or no value, and if a special person or persons doesn't have the affection for one of these animals, then it has to search and travel the streets for food, for shelter, for water, with love nowhere in sight. Then one day they might be picked up off the street and put in a cage, still not fed and watered properly. If no one comes to claim or adopt him or her, their days of life are shortened exponentially from what their natural life would have offered if spent living with a loving, caring family.

Perhaps this is why I've always cherished unwanted pets, or have

---

1 Personal Justice Denied, the report by the Commission on Wartime Relocation and Internment of Civilians, 1982.

cheered endlessly for "David character" facing against goliaths or any other heavily favored giant.

Lucky was stolen from the car, near this area.
This path through the Mangroves leads to the Estuary
at Bahia Delfin of the Sea of Cortez.

3. A Lucky Beginning in Mexico

I found Lucky in a brown, weather-beaten cardboard box one morning about six years ago as I left my vehicle to go inside Rosa's Cantina for breakfast with my ex-wife. A Mexican man came up to me and showed me the tiny dog that lay cuddled in a corner of the cardboard carrier. He mentioned something to me about buying Lucky from him, but I dismissed the notion as we had two dogs with us already–Princess, a Pekingese and Gigi, a Pomeranian. As we enjoyed that morning meal, our talk included the subject of the little pup in the box and if perhaps we should take the dog. After eating some delicious food, we went back out and found the box was now closed, the four flaps had been overlapped, and there lying was little Lucky, hot and sleepy, still curled up in a corner. I picked up the box and was putting it in the vehicle when the man came running over to our car, breathlessly demanding that we couldn't take the dog. I pulled a twenty-dollar bill from my pocket and handed it to the man. An English, "Okay" came from his heavily accented Mexican tongue and we had a new pup. The little guy was about six weeks of age, and he was a white, tiny, furry bundle of fun.

Did I find Lucky or did Lucky find me? This has always been a question unanswered as my *perro* (dog) buddy has given me great companionship and loyalty these past half a dozen years.

Lucky was smuggled across the border as an illegal canine because we were scheduled to leave the next day back to Temecula, California. I thought that if I took Lucky to a veterinarian to get checked out and shots taken before leaving, he would be put in some sort of quarantine for a week or at least a few days before being allowed into the States. The two of us made a decision that we would smuggle our newfound Mexican amigo over the border into Nogales, Arizona. Two hours before getting to the border we did everything possible to keep Lucky awake, busy, and using stored energy because the pup wanted to do nothing but sleep. About twenty miles from Nogales, we pulled the car over and let Lucky curl up to rest, covered him in some blankets in a well-hidden area of the back seat amongst various articles of clothing, beach towels, suitcases, a bottle of tequila, a small cooler and a sack of snacks all covering up the illegal alien that slept peacefully and soundly. If our little Lucky was discovered by the agents, we would receive a hefty fine and be turned away at the border to return home.

We had the other two dogs join us in the front seat so that when we were waved up by the Border Patrol officer, all the officer would see was a madhouse near the driver's and passenger seat. As we rolled up, the officer saw two humans fidgeting nervously, while two dogs jumped, hopped, and scurried from anxiousness, and everything in between. The last thing he was looking for was another pet as he had us roll all windows down and did a quick "grab this and turn over that" inspection. We held our breaths in hope that the little, white doggie would not be awakened and yip as the officer's hands were within reach of our hidden, undeclared merchandise. The border agent handed us back our passports and told us to have a good day. I was so nervous that I nearly pushed the pedal completely to the floorboard. I am sure rubber was laid on the pavement that day.

And so it began, my life with Lucky.

We had been coming down quite often to San Carlos as we were having a house built on the hill at Esmeralda Bahia just above the new marina in San Carlos. Nueva Marina was located on the backside of Tetakawi Mountain, the symbolic and iconic mountain of which San Carlos is known for. The backdrop of Tetakawi Mountain was so named by the indigenous Indians of the Yaqui people. Tetakawi looks like two upside-down goat teats (from which its name originates) as you enter into San Carlos from the main road, that of highway 15. In Spanish, Tetakawi is *"tetra de la cabra"* which translated into English is "teat of the goat." Tetakawi was once the sacred landmark of San Carlos; but, now due to the high price of ocean and marina view property being what it is, Tetakawi Mountain is now sprinkled with home sites and multimillion dollar, expansive homes with negative edge pools and all the other luxuries that many millions of pesos can afford.

San Carlos with its beauty and friendly locals had drawn us into making the decision to build our vacation home there. In fact, National Geographic named the area of Mirador Escenico, San Carlos, Mexico as having the most scenic ocean view in its book, *Secret Journeys of a Lifetime*. It ranked #1 of its top 10 locations in the world, topping beautiful destinations such as Kalaupapa, Molokai, Hawaii that garnered second place with Cape Leeuwin, Australia and Sur to Aja, Oman, rounding out number three and four respectively, followed closing at number five by Látrabjarg, Iceland. The next five that were included in the Top 10 were just as impressive with selections from all over the globe.

Here is what National Geographic wrote in a 2011 travel article titled, "Top 10 Ocean Views" about the place where Lucky was born and where I am lucky to reside part-time:

"This scenic lookout, four miles from San Carlos, gives a peerless view over the Gulf of California, dramatic Tetakawi, a volcanic hill jutting out of the sea and the secluded coves of Playa Piedras Pintas. Mirador is also a world-class vantage point for spotting wildlife, including dolphins, pelicans, and whales. A good way to explore the Gulf of California (Sea of Cortez) is to rent a kayak or fishing boat in San Carlos. The best sailing and fishing weather occurs from November through May."[1]

We've never found a more beautiful spot in our lives and it seemed that others were in agreement. So, from that day forward when we found Lucky, he with our other two dogs traveled back and forth with us during the construction phase. We would usually rent a condo at Marina Terra, located at the original marina. Marina Terra also has a hotel directly adjacent to the condos, separated by a view fence, each with its own large swimming pool and Jacuzzi.

Before our dream home overlooking the Nueva Marina was built, we had lost the other two members of our dog family due to old age and cancer. So upon finally moving in, it was truly Lucky's home and sanctuary.

When Lucky first came up missing, I had hoped it was a practical joke by some Mexican kids that wanted the beer, wine and food left in our car, or that perhaps an American or Canadian had seen my white pooch alone in the car and decided to give me a little lesson (even though it was not hot out that day) as I took a quick stroll to look at the estuary. I soon ruled out the lesson theory, as other items in the car had been taken along with

1 https://www.nationalgeographic.com/travel/article/ocean-views

Lucky. After looking and searching and calling out his name for four hours, darkness had completely enveloped the community of San Carlos. When we could no longer see anything but the blackness of the dark night, Letty and I finally called it quits for the evening. I sobbed when I returned home after dropping my dear friend Letty off at her residence. The next morning I could tell that Letty too had cried and cried for our lost, little amigo by her partially swollen eyes, which were tired-looking and red.

Our day the next morning began with driving through the dirt streets and back roads of the town that I had loved for many years, and now I was beginning to slowly dislike them. San Carlos was looking distant and lonely even though most of the residents and shop owners of whom we spoke, each gladly responded, that an eager eye would be looking for Lucky.

I had a repetitious phrase that I would ask each person: "Please keep your eyes open for a poofy, white hair, poodle mix. He stands one foot and six inches in height, weighs approximately 13 pounds, and is about five years old. He was last seen wearing a red collar with a bow and has 'Disneyland' tags. Lucky has also been given a chip." Lucky had a microchip implant that is an identifying integrated circuit that was placed just under his skin. It was about the size of a large grain of rice and I could feel it on occasion when I would pet Lucky. In the U.S., animal shelters, animal control officers (dog catchers), and veterinarians routinely look for the microchip as a way to return a lost pet quickly to its family. I didn't know how prevalent this method was or was not used in Mexico.

I had Postcards printed with Lucky's picture and the number to call should a person find or see Lucky. Half of the Postcard was written in English, the other half was in Spanish. Letty and I were placing them on all the car windows, in storefronts, on doors and handing them out almost as fast as the printer was producing the colorful, lost-and-found placards.

It was now March 4th and still, I was no closer to finding Lucky than I had been four days earlier when I had walked away from my car with Lucky sitting quietly inside. I knew that I had to take a marketing approach to locate my dog for a successful reunion. I understood marketing as I had studied it at Pepperdine University while working on my unfinished degree. (I have two businesses that are doing fantastic in sales volume because I have marketed them both extremely well and I have an excellent product.) Lucky was now my excellent product of which I needed to get safely home to me. Instead of selling or distributing, I concentrate on buying or receiving something of great, undisclosed value. Lucky was my boy and I would do everything in my power to bring him back home; I knew he had to be terrified and possibly depressed.

I hired two Mexican men to help me in my search: Armando, a man from Guaymas and with a heart of gold, and Jesus, a much-smaller man of physical stature with a teardrop tattoo streaming down his cheek. Jesus had the appearance of someone rugged and mean and was from Tijuana. Both Jesus and Armando were gentle souls, but, if things were to get rough, I had no doubt they would be the ones who would still be standing after a battle to protect me.

I also had Letty looking full-time. I would strategize with my helpers and sometimes one or two of them would ride with me to canvas an area or I would drop them off in a certain part of a city, such as Guaymas, and I would drive to another section of the city to talk with people in the street and hand out flyers. A few times I would even send them on the bus to different neighboring towns or to a further remote part of the city. At first, my helpers were only interested in the money aspect of it, but after a few days into it, perhaps it was seeing my attitude, persistence, and love toward finding Lucky, I could tell their work ethic changed much for the better. I now could see their hearts were completely into helping me find my lost and stolen friend.

"Team Lucky"
Armando, Jesus
& Jim.

Armando working the
shopping district of Guaymas.

Letty, constantly searching for Lucky from day one.

Alvaro aka "Big Al," helping Jim with a search plan.

4 🐾 Viva San Carlos! A Blog to Save the Life of a Dog

Viva San Carlos[1] was my next step in finding Lucky as it is a website with a community bulletin board. Viva San Carlos is the guide to all things in San Carlos, Sonora, Mexico on the Sea of Cortez.

Before a person can register and be admitted into the site, they are overly encouraged to read the rules which begin:

"A community board for residents and visitors to Guaymas/San Carlos Mexico. Mexico is a land of enchantment. However, it is very different from the U.S. and Canada. This is the place to explore those differences. If you want to help or give information about specific subjects to prepare for an enjoyable visit, to avoid instead of inviting problems, then share experiences and tips. THIS IS THE PLACE! And remember what you say will also be seen by others and possibly answered by them. If you make a mistake just re-enter; incorrect entries will be deleted."

On March 5th after having been approved access and newly registered on Viva San Carlos, I entered my first Post.

Note: In order to show the overwhelming help and support I received, I have elected to share the Posts. I have changed a few of the usernames if it was too close to their personal names or had their last name attached. I have used my name (Jim) instead of my username for ease of understanding. I will list the date at the beginning of the first Post of that day.

Day 5 - March 5th
Post 1: Jim - On Saturday, March 1, around 4 p.m. I

---

1 Viva San Carlos' vivasancarlos.mx has a Community Bulletin Board: A Friendly Place to Share What's Happening in San Carlos

was visiting the estuary next to Condo Pilar with my dear "Lucky." It was a mild night and I could not bring "Lucky" so I left the windows down a bit, locked the doors and went on my walk. Half way in, I heard my alarm go off and did not arrive back in time. "Lucky" was gone. So, please keep your eyes open for a poofy, white hair poodle mix. About 13 pounds, stands 1' 6" and he is 5 years old. Wearing red collar with bow and has "Disneyland" tags. Lucky also has been "chipped". He may be shaved now so please keep your eyes out.

Thanks, Jim US 951 xxx xxxx Mexico: Letty 622 xxx xx xx

Post 2: FishingSanCarlos – Keep looking Jim

Post 3: PT - Will keep my eyes open, so sad that people need to steal a dog.

Post 4: Jim - Still working diligently and faithfully. Miss my buddy.

Post 5: WyYnot - I think it's really neat to see the big "traveling banner" from near the old marina to down past Charlies Rock. Also the little postcard type pictures on all the cars. Someone is looking very hard, and we will certainly watch and look. I have a question on the chip. How does it work down here? I thought they were scanned by satellite, maybe not so, "they"/whoever implanted can't trace their chip? Ron

Post 6: IronwoodChef – I cannot believe some **No Good Dirty Lousy Scumbag Person** would break into someone's car to steal someone's pet. I Hope The Person meets a very Painful END Soon.

Post 7: Jim - Thanks for your support and a very kind

thanks to Viva San Carlos. Still hunting on the streets. Tomorrow I'll be in Guaymas.

Post 8: Jim - Hi Ron and thanks for your reply. I called "Home Again" the chip company/service. There are no gas units / tracking implants at this time, only chips for scanning. I have called them and reported the loss. The good news, any veterinarian who scans this will receive a report that "Lucky" has been reported missing and the central data base will be alerted. I hope I find him soon. Thanks, Jim

Post 9: Daisy - Hoping to hear news that you are reunited with Lucky!

Post 10: VinoBlanco - Go to the man who runs the bus schedule just east of Fiesta Hotel by the Condos Triana, bus stop under the big tree. He has helped others find dogs by posting on the bus, your information.

Post 11: Jim - Hi Everyone. Still no "Lucky." Today I posted more banners and had people standing on the main road with signs. It's been a difficult and unbelievable road. Tomorrow we're going into Guaymas and Miramar to start "working" that area. There will only be one person out here and the manpower is going to be shifted there for a couple of days, and come back here and then alternate.

I've contacted most vets here locally, contacted the guy at the bus stop (but I'm going to hang out there tomorrow and hand them out too), door knocking, interrupted people at breakfast, lunch and dinner, visited and posted at the place of loss, talked to people on the streets, police officers and put flyers on cars. Does anyone have any other ideas that can help?

Thanks for your attention, patience for talking with me, tolerating the flyers on your cars, being another set of eyes for me and especially for your kind thoughts and prayers for

"Lucky." Out on the streets tomorrow. Will keep you posted. Thanks, Jim

Post 12: HippieHappy - I can put the photo on my Facebook?

Post 13: Jim - Sure! That would be very appreciated. If you pass your email to me, I'll send it over to you. Thanks for your kind consideration, Jim

Post 14: HippieHappy – hippiehappy@xxxxx

Post 15: DonJaime - LET THEM KNOW HOW MUCH THE REWARD IS!!!! IT IS ALL ABOUT THE MONEY!!!
Dog napping happens in SC, more than you would think. You need to offer a substantial reward, and get the word out. About the "no questions ask" reward. The guy around the bus stop has worked in the past. Put your flyers up with a substantial Reward. The sooner, the better.

Post 16: PT - Just copy and save the picture above and you can share it on your own FB page. I just did it on mine with some explanation about it.

Post 17: DonJaime - THEY WANT MONEY! Make your best offer. FB in SC!

Day 6 - March 6th
Post 18: Lourdes - I LOVE YOU AMORSITO! Also Lucky, thanks you for ALL YOUR HARD WORK! When James (Jim) would say "I love you" to Lucky, Lucky would say it back (it's true, no fish stories- PROMISE!) Those two would be howling "I love you" to each other- it's SO ADORABLE! If you see my James (Jim) on the street, ask him if he has eaten, with all this, mi AMORSITO is for-

getting to eat! Sincerely, Lourdes P.

(Author's note) - Jim and Lourdes are sharing the same Viva San Carlos account so Lourdes will make it a point to let others know that she is Posting at those times instead of Jim. Lourdes was at her home in Southern California.

Post 19: Jim - Good Morning folks. Off to another day to hunt for "Lucky." Please pray and wish the best. Jim

Post 20: WyYnot - I agree with Don Jaime, post a "NO QUESTIONS ASKED" healthy reward, so all can see. Suggest some pesos to the old timer at the bus stop if he helps your success. Maybe talk to the guys in blue here and in Guaymas. Email Victor L. (Bulldog) who now works in Guaymas. Our new Policia Turistica with their quads, stop and visit with everyone. Again, we'll certainly help watch and wish you a happy outcome! Ron

Post 21: HippieHappy - ;-) with a thumbs up!

Post 22: Jim – WyYnot, good suggestions. I posted a large reward on Guaymas website and instructing people to hand out the cards and mention "Large". Miramar and Guaymas is our focus today. I'll try to find "Bulldog" and talk with him. Going to personally stand at bus stop for awhile and pass out cards. Thanks.

Post 23: Panchita - Call the TV news program called MEGANOTICIAS, they often mention lost dogs and their owners phone numbers. It is on the mega cable channel and during the program they give out their phone number to call the show.

Post 24: Jim - Thanks! Lourdes, can you contact this station in Guaymas and ask for help. Look this up on the

Internet for more information.

Post 25: Lourdes - Good morning everyone, this is Lourdes P., James' girlfriend. I called Meganoticias this morning & they will be posting Lucky's picture for all to see! Once again, thank you all for your support!

Post 26: Panchita - Also if you haven't done so yet, call the radio stations too. They also announce lost pets.

Post 27: Lourdes - Hola Panchita, this is Lourdes, I would like to thank you & everyone for your wonderful ideas! Panchita, what radio station is it? I'm helping via California, I just need the name and I will do the rest 😊. Thanks a bunch, Lourdes P.

P.S. My James is still out looking for Lucky, please continue to pray for him & the other people in this effort to find our little guy!

Post 28: Jim - Good Evening everyone. I just walked into the house from a long day. Posted more banners, had "Lucky" announced on 90.1, twice. He will also be in a classified 3"x3" ad in a Guaymas newspaper that will run Friday through Sunday. Also, on the television station as suggested - Meganoticias, Ricardo Forte was kind enough to listen to the story and consider the TV spot. (Thanks Lourdes!) Printed more handouts, walked and talked. The working team (Team Lucky) is just great. Any more ideas?

Thanks for your support and following my posts. It means everything. Jim Kawaguchi

Post 29: GeorgeInSanCarlos - Do not give up. We just got this email from a friend:

"We just returned from a three week trip mostly to southern Arizona, mostly very nice. I say, 'mostly,' because Blanquita (blind and deaf, as you probably remember) disappeared from our boondock campsite just south of Why, AZ. We composed a flier with a color picture and description and phone numbers, leaving them everywhere we could imagine would be even remotely effective. After three days and three nights with no word, we felt there was no hope and reluctantly, tearfully, and in grief, headed toward home. We had driven about two hours to Wickenburg when I checked messages on our cell phone. I couldn't believe my ears. There were messages from a Border Patrol agent and from the Ajo animal control shelter that Blanquita had been found (probably about four miles from our campsite) and was at the Ajo shelter. We immediately left our trailer in Wickenburg and high tailed it back to Ajo. We're still somewhat incredulous that she came back to us.

Spring is in the air here with (undoubtedly) more winter showing itself now and then. Looking forward to hearing from you." Warmly, Larry R. and Cheryl I.

Post 30: Panchita - Lourdes, here is a page with a list of about 6 radio stations. Try them and see if they might post it. Good luck!

http://tunein.com/radio/Guaymas-r101468/

Day 7 - March 7ᵗʰ

Post 31: Lourdes - Good morning, this is Lourdes, James' (Jim) girlfriend. George, thanks for your support we are very hopeful, I'm sure your story will rejuvenate James, as he & Team Lucky head out on another 12 hour day. Panchita, thank you for the radio stations, I will be all over that today ☺! God bless all of you, Lourdes

Post 32: Jim - Good Morning! Today could be "Lucky's" lucky day. My hopes say it's so and I'm ready to go. Coffee, a little breakfast and I'm off again. Guaymas and Miramar, Walmart area and into Miramar again. Please keep your prayers going. Thanks, Jim Kawaguchi

Post 33: Jim - These are the recent shots of Lucky. The black and white is going to be in the newspaper today through Sunday. The other picture is of him actually being on TV.

(Author's note) – Jim had attached two images of Lucky (1) offering a $500 reward without questions and (2) the other of Lucky's photo on television.

Post 34: WyYnot - WOW, if that's not the better part of $6500 pesos then my calculator's broke. Best of "LUCK" today and hope it's a "Lucky" Friday. I'll bet you have lots of eyes watching and searching. Ron

Post 35: Jim - Oh boy, Lucky is worth every bit of that reward!

Post 36: Jim - Almost 1p.m. and no Lucky yet. Looked at 2 dogs so far today and no match.

Post 37: Daisy - Are there posters up in Empalme?

Post 38: PT - Just shared it again on my FB page. Let's hope that this will be the day, it's still not over yet.

Post 39: Lourdes - Hello everyone, this is Lourdes, I've been in communication with Meganoticias and they will be posting Lucky's picture nightly! Thank you Ricardo

Post 40: MaryPh - Hope you get Lucky back.

Post 41: Jim - "Lucky" had another spot on TV today and will be shown the next four days. This was donated air by Meganoticias. Thank you! On Monday I have a mobile 8'x4' banner with sound featuring the voice of a local DJ from 90.1 (who also donated his efforts -Fernando!) announcing the search for "Lucky." Thank you! The same radio station donated four bits of air time as well and mentions he'll do it for as long as we need. Huge thanks again!

Today, we were again in Guaymas and Miramar. My team is showing sincere effort now, as they really want to find Lucky too. It's more than work now. They are getting thumbs up and Guaymas seems to be paying attention.

Tomorrow, I'm going to take the advice of Daisy and move a person to Empalme. Hung another sign on a fence in Miramar which seemed to be a very popular beachside bar/restaurant with a child's park/ slides next to it. Handed flyers out in that neighborhood as well. Thanks for your support. Jim Kawaguchi (with attached picture of Lucky on television)

Post 42: Panchita - Don't forget to put up some lost signs/posters in Guaymas Norte area.

Post 43: Jim - Panchitas, I had a team member there at the entrance. I also had a lead there too which wwasnt (sic) Lucky. Gave the newspaper guy (at the entrance of Guamas (sic) Norte) a few pesos to insert flyers in the newspapers. More ideas! Thanks, keep them coming.

Post 44: Jim - I'm very tired, sorry about my spelling.

Photo from post 1.

RECOMPENSA!! REWARD!! "LUCKY"

Poodle mixto Poodle mix
Collar rojo con moño
Red collar w/bow
Perdido en Cond. Pilar, Estero del Soldado, San Carlos.

$500 dlls.
SIN PREGUNTAS!!
NO QUESTIONS!!

CALL. (622) 109 53 78
JIM. 951-491-9182
LETTY. (622) 115 17 80
or U.S. 951-693-4849

Post 33.

Post 33 photo 2.

Post 44.

5  Week Two is Upon Us

During my first week of searching for Lucky, becoming organized and accepting the outpouring of human generosity kept me from thinking too much about how lonely my little guy must have been. Each night I hit the pillow hard as I had been running on adrenaline most of the day and into the evenings, forgetting to eat, not taking my medication as prescribed. I truly believed that Lucky would be back in my arms before the end of too many more days as I could already feel the vibe of the Guaymas and San Carlos population wanting to find out who might win the lottery of $6,500 pesos with Lucky in hand. As much as I hated paying a thief who stole Lucky, I knew it would possibly be the only way that I would be reunited with my world as it was before his disappearance.

Ever since I was a teenage boy, I spent most of my life with a dog as my companion. Never had I lost a dog by theft. Before, my furry friends had always left me from either old age, or because cancer had developed in their bodies near the end of their last dog days. No matter how old the dog was when he or she died, it was always hard, even though I had seen the warning signs of their tail wagging nearing a final close. However, Lucky was only six years old and in great health and I figured I still had possibly ten more great years of his wonderful company.

With all the time spent searching for Lucky, I reminisced about the fun times I'd enjoyed with this dog and other dogs that had been a part of my life. My first dog had been paid for through money that I had found. I was sixteen years of age and had purchased a boat that was made in 1957, originally designed for Roy Rogers. My fascination and number one priority as a teenager had not been a car, but, a boat. While all my other friends had been saving their hard-earned money for their first car, I had saved my din-ero for a boat to take my two younger brothers, ages ten and fourteen, and myself out fishing. My mother allowed me to buy a trailer hitch for her car and I would tow my boat behind a Cadillac Coupe de Ville to the Redondo Beach Harbor.

One summer day in 1977 after a super day of fishing, my brothers and I had loaded the boat onto the trailer and were busy wiping her down when I spotted a green wad of cash lying on a nearby large rock. Four hundred dollars. Yes, there were twenty twenty-dollar bills just waiting to be picked up! Red's Bait & Tackle was nearby, so my two brothers and I walked to the shop and told the manager about our find. The shop keeper told us that he would hold onto the money and if no one came in the next hour, the claim would be all mine. My brothers and I were nervously watching from a distance as each customer walked in and out of the shop, wondering if the money had been taken back by the poor soul who had lost their money. As the minutes slowly ticked by, sixty of them had finally made their way around the time piece and we eagerly entered Red's again. The money had not been claimed and was presented back to my hands. I took a twenty from the twenty bills and gave the honest store keeper a twenty-dollar bill.

I knew what I was going to do with the money. A Chinese Chow Chow had caught my eye a week earlier, but I did not have the $300 asking price. However, now my fate had been altered by a great find next to the Pacific Ocean.

The Chow is a dog breed originally from northern China, where it is referred to as *Songshi Quan* which means "puffy-lion dog." The breed has also been called the *Tang Quan*, "Dog of the Tang Empire." It has long been believed that the Chow Chow is one of the native dogs used as the model for the Foo Dog, the traditional stone guardians found in front of Buddhist temples and palaces. It is one of the few ancient dog breeds still in existence in the world today, and I wanted one. See Gee was ten weeks old when I bought her for $300. With the other $80 bucks, I purchased lots of dog food.

This girl died twelve years later and I cried for my friend, who was also my first dog. Many things had happened during those 12 years, incredi-bly, good things and some things not so great and pleasant, but one thing remained constant–my love for See Gee and the impact of her unwavering devotion and love for me.

My time with Lucky had been half as many years, and as I thought of the dogs in my life, a memory in the form of a wet tear, slowly ran down my cheek as I waited for the stoplight to change from a glowing red to an emerald green in Guaymas, Sonora, Mexico.

Day 8 - March 8ᵗʰ

Post 45: bobnliz – Sure hope you find "Lucky" and he lives up to his name. We will keep a lookout for him. Lizzy

Post 46: Jim - Thank you Lizzy, getting started today. I'm really hoping that with everything, we reach a good crowd of people with the banners and media.

Prayers. Prayers. Have a nice day everyone.

Post 47: Jim - (with attached picture of Lucky and reward)

Post 48: Lourdes - Good morning, this is Lourdes, don't lose hope mi amor! I love you♡♡

Post 49: Jim - Just received a phone call from a person in Hermosillo who said "they don't want to get in trouble, but knows who took it and where the dog is." This may be the big break we need. Please pray and cross your fingers. We will start discussions at 6 p.m.

Post 50: Dweller - We are all praying for you & Lucky, hope you have good news.

Post 51: Lourdes - This is Lourdes P., WOW WOW WOW!

Post 52: Jim - Good Evening. I walked away from today's experience a little confused and I'm not sure if I did the right thing.

This is what happened. I received a phone call today from someone advising me they knew where Lucky was (Hermosillo) and that they were working and could not talk. Ninety minutes later we called and the line almost sounded like a fax machine or Internet line and the communication was very difficult to hear or make out. At that time he made it clear that Lucky was not in Hermosillo, but in Guaymas.

I questioned this and he mentioned as a result of phone credit he could not talk, but only text, so our communication commenced by finger. After a couple of texts he made it clear he needed a small amount of money to be put on his phone so we could chat. Easy enough, I was in Guaymas Norte and went to the nearest OXXO. (Their store placements are odd and areas seem saturated).

When I went to put the money on the phone, their number was declined. I then double checked the number and it was correct. I then left confused. I then started thinking if this was on the "up and up." I started up my car and drove off wondering what the hell was going on. Being late I started my drive back to San Carlos and then we started receiving texts from the same guy, but, from another phone.

He started questioning us about Lucky and the phone and then we fired back, "send us a picture," and then he replied, "I don't have a way to." I believed that this could be very possible and then mentioned the reward ($500.00 dollars) and to meet us. He mentioned Guaymas and I replied: (without disclosing the place of Lucky's loss), "Please meet us where you all found him." He replied. "Listen, I don't know where they found him, I just know it's your dog." I replied, "It's $500.00 dollars, so find a way to notify me and send a picture." While all this was going on I started thinking this could be a "set up" and possibly put us both in a very bad situation. Being a little unsure, I declined to go forward to search for this guy in Guaymas.

Please everyone, I'm not sure if I was wrong or right in this situation, but I do know I would really like some feedback.

If there are any active or retired police / law enforcement officers here in town that may have experience or are trained for these situations, I would really like to sit down for a cup of coffee and discuss what to ask and what to refrain from asking. Also, how to negotiate in the event it comes back to this, and how to settle this safely.

Somehow, I thought today with all the media exposure, would turn over a rock. Oh well. In God's timing, I pray for Lucky's safe return. With your help, we can do this. Thanks, Jim Kawaguchi

Post 53: Mary - I'm wondering if the person who called was in prison and trying to run a scam. That might explain why the number was declined. I think you did the right thing.

Post 54: Jim – Thanks, Mary. Stomach is in knots. It's been a week now.

Post 55: T Bird Richard - Whatever you do, DO NOT meet anyone related to this without law enforcement personnel with you! I think you did the right thing. Some years ago, a prominent SC businessman agreed to meet a person offering to buy the car that the businessman had for sale. The meeting, logically enough, was set up at a bank parking lot. They met, and he was kidnapped. Richard B.

Post 56: Jim - Richard, Thanks for your advice and I will take it. Please keep your thoughts coming. Jim Kawaguchi

Day 9 - March 9ᵗʰ
Post 57: Jim - Good morning, today may be the day! Hitting Guaymas, Empalme, La Manga and later, El Mirador. Remember, I'll take any advice. This a picture of Lucky 2 months ago with his mohawk. Miss my buddy. Please keep Lucky in your hearts. (attached picture of Lucky)

Post 58: Fantome - Oh, the Mohawk is hilarious! What a sport Lucky is. Good luck getting him back safely, for both of you.

Post 59: Lourdes - Hello this is Lourdes. Amor what a SUPER picture of Lucky, this is Lucky's normal look, he's very stylish! Have an amazing day my sweet!

Post 60: Chef66 - We saw a dog fitting the description in the parking lot at La Perla in Guaymas around noon on Saturday.

Post 61: FishingSanCarlos - We are praying too, Jim. So sorry. Jennifer and John

Post 62: Jim - Hi everyone and thanks for your support. Well no "Lucky" today. I know the routine well and the team members are easy to manage as they are familiar with Lucky and what has to be done. I'm "lucky" to have them. Tonight when I was driving home I realized how quiet my life is now. Lucky sure kept me company and made me laugh. I'm really starting to miss the bond.

Whatever the case, keeping my chin up and hitting the streets again tomorrow.

Your thoughts and prayers are appreciated. Thanks, Jim Kawaguchi

Post 63: Susan - You probably have no idea how many people are watching your posts, waiting for the word that you have been reunited with your little dog. Every time I see a post from you, I click on it, thinking, "this is it, this is it." You have done everything humanly possible. I have confidence that your hard work and love will bring you back with your boy. SS

Post 64: Jim - Thanks Susan! Your comment is so very

nice. I'm not sure of the amount of followers with Lucky, but I am committed to posting as it helps me through this process and I feel there is some interest. When I hear a nice, uplifting comment like yours or a private message, it sure helps with restoring my confidence and goal. With warmest wishes, Jim

Day 10 – March 10ᵗʰ

Post 65: Maggy - Me too Jim, am praying you get your precious dog back. I have a special pooch also, she is 15 and 3 months, and I know the time is coming when she will go to doggie heaven. Your dog is around somewhere, keep positive and hopeful, and let us know soon that she is back home with you.

Post 66: Jim - Maggy, Good morning and thanks for your wishes. Give your poodle a hug for me and have a great day. Jim

Post 67: Dweller - Believe it, there are many people following your pursuit. It is on my morning agenda to check to see if this is the day. I look at my little Yorkie and would be lost without her, so can relate to your anguish. Keep looking, and we will keep praying.

Post 68: Mathis47 - My husband and I follow your post every day hoping you will find Lucky. It is the very first thing we do in the morning when we get up, and the last thing we do before bed. This is just a bit of information that might or might not be of any help, but when we were going back to AZ week before last, we were approached by a man in Santa Ana wanting to sell us a gorgeous German Shepherd puppy about 7 months old for $15. We could not buy him because we were heading through customs and had no paperwork on him. I'm sure he was stolen. Just some information I thought might be added to the mix. We are keeping our fingers crossed that Lucky will be rescued.

Day 11 – March 11th

Post 69: Hello this is Lourdes, we are all praying for Lucky's safe return amor. Just got off the phone with James, he tells me there was a sighting of Lucky! It was in Guaymas, Lucky had his red collar on, looking very dirty and was underneath a bus bench at Soriana. When the man approached Lucky he was very skittish, due to his unfamiliar surroundings and bolted! So everyone, we now have a good lead, & TEAM LUCKY WILL BE ALL OVER THIS LIKE WHITE ON RICE! Give me a T, give me a E, give me a A, give me a M, and give me a L, give me a U, give me a C, give me a K, give me a Y! Go Go Go JAMES WE LOVE YOU AMORSITO! Dos besos ♥♥♡♥♡♥♡♥♡

Post 70: Sylvie - Hello Jim, I would like to join Team Lucky. Any time you need another hand to check out leads, call me. 226-xxx. One time my Indy Boy was lost for 6 hours until he came hobbling back at midnight. Never found out what happened to him, but I never want to feel that pain again. Praying every day your Lucky is found.

Post 71: Lourdes - Sylvie this is Lourdes, I enjoyed your story it makes me very hopeful for Lucky ☺!

Post 72: Jim - Good evening everyone. No Lucky today. We worked the Soriana Market area today. Had the banners up and handed out flyers. I drove up and down streets, calling for my little buddy and looking inside drains and under stairways for possible retreats. Today I presented new flyers with the new reward amount of $1000.00, and to the radio station, 90.1 FM. I know the original amount was a lot of money; however, considering the rising temperatures, the possibility of little or no food or water over several days, I needed to do this.

Tomorrow I understand there will be a swap meet in central Guaymas, where a large sum of people gather to trade and shop. I'm going to position a Team Lucky member there to talk and hand out flyers. I have to hand it to Armando, one of the "Team Lucky" members. He works hard and is excited and motivated to find Lucky. Tonight when I arrived to have supplies returned for the day, it so happened that the DJ from 90.1 was chatting on the radio about Lucky. It not only uplifted me, but put a smile on Armando's face. Armando just smiled, raised his fist and said; "We'll find him Jim." It just about brought me to tears. (I'm going to save those for the day I get my buddy back). Another person will be working the neighborhoods surrounding the Soriana Market and I'll be working the bus stations reposting the reward changes on all banners. Also, I felt to help minimize the expense of someone trying to help Lucky and communicate with me, I created a toll-free number and printed it on the new flyers. All phone calls are forwarded to my California office, where I have an employee able and ready to help.

Also, Sylvie that is a really nice offer; however, I really want you to think about the exposure and the areas I'm working right now. They are really busy areas where you have to be on your toes. Helping me out in San Carlos would be great!

I'm tired and going to bed. Good night everyone.

AOK. Last, my office received a phone call from a local television station inquiring about an interview with me about Lucky. I found this very interesting as the story on Lucky is starting to reach many, and is being well accepted by the City of Guaymas and surrounding areas.

Post 74: jmjphx - We have been following your story about Lucky. We will continue to follow it until we hear good news. We wish you all the luck in the world!

Post 75: Traveler - Is the word out in Obregon?

Post 76: Panchita - Did you check around the Soriana store on the corner of Serdan and 10th Street?

Post 77: Jim – Traveler, other than what they may have heard on the radio or TV, no. My vehicle does not have the right permits for me; however, I need to talk about this with Letty. That's a good idea. Thanks!

Post 78: Jim - Panchita, I'm not sure of the location of the Soriana store I've been working. I go there by memory. It's off the main road into Guaymas and to the right (Industrial) and a little drive down that road. Let me know if that is where you are thinking of. Thanks, Jim

Day 12 – March 12th
Post 79: Jim - Good morning!

Post 80: Panchita - It sounds like you are going to the Soriana store on Benito Juarez. There is another one on Serdan, at the corner of Calle 10. It has an underground parking lot. When you come into Guaymas, stay on the main street and continue to where the road splits into a Y (there is a fountain and an obelisk). Stay to your right on the street that says "centro." You will come to a set of lights on Calle 10 and you'll see the Soriana store on the corner. I would check the various parks in centro also, ask the guys who wash cars, they see a lot of stuff.

Post 81: SanCarlosMaverick - Jim, I live in Obregon and would be happy to post and hand out flyers at the high traffic points here. I also can have our maid hand out flyers to all of the buses that transport the locals throughout the city. Trust me, the locals know EVERYTHING that goes on in the city. All I would need is someone that can bring the flyers south and I can meet them at Walmart, which is on the north end of Obregon. Let me know if you need my help. Mark

P.S. A suggestion for your next run of flyers would be to post the reward in pesos ($13,000 MXN), rather than dollars. It's easier for the locals to relate to pesos than dollars.

Post 82: Jim - Santa Fe, would it be OK if we send package by Tufesa to you? If so, we'll ship package today.

Post 83: Jim - That message was for "Maverick."

Post 84: Lourdes - This is Lourdes, my prayers go with you as you venture out into Guaymas.♡□♡□♡□

Post 85: Jim – Maverick, just had new flyers printed with $13,000 pesos. Good idea. I can ship them today on Tufesa. Let me know please.

Post 86: Jim - Heading to Empalme right now. A possible sighting.

Post 87: Lourdes - Hello Maverick, this is Lourdes, James' girlfriend, thanks for your kindness, concern and the good idea about the pesos. Most of all, your help getting the word out about our little guy LUCKY!

Post 88: Lourdes - This is Lourdes. WOW - amor may GOD be with you and give you STRENGTH as you set out for this new sighting of LUCKY! I LOVE YOU AMORSITO

Post 89: repost by Lourdes - This is Lourdes. WOW - amor may GOD be with you and give you STRENGTH as you set out for this new sighting of LUCKY! I LOVE YOU AMORSITO

Post 90: Jim – SanCarlosMaverick, what would you like me to do?

Post 91: Jim - We had two very close matches. One was in central Empalme and the other in San Vicente area of Guaymas. The pooch in San Vicente was almost exact, but did not respond to me and had huge juevos. My dog is fixed.

Post 92: SanCarlosMaverick - Jim, sent you a PM.

Post 93: Lourdes - Hello everyone, this is Lourdes, just got off phone with James. No Lucky today. Their search took them into Guaymas - San Vicente and Barrio. They looked at three dogs today and one was in Empalme. They were all similar, but none of them ran towards James in recognition 😊. They ended the day at 7 p.m. and tomorrow they will be working in Obregon. We would like to give a special thanks to Maverick for his kind help in Obregon. Good night Team Lucky

Day 13 – March 13th
Post 94: Jim - Good morning everyone, I hope you all have a nice day and that today is my "Lucky" day. Jim

Post 95: Jim - Hi Everyone, just left from visiting this pooch. He was dressed up for me. I was impressed with the effort and drove away with a smile. Not Lucky, but the calls keep coming. Thanks for your support. Jim (with attached photo of not Lucky)

Post 96: Mary - Was anything else taken from your car? Was your car damaged or were they able to break in a more sophisticated manner? A dog napper would usually be looking for the ads and would respond quite rapidly. This is a very odd case. $500 is a huge reward down here. It's hard to imagine someone having the dog and not jumping to claim it. Now people are probably trying to pawn their own dogs for the money. Is there any chance someone would have felt you should not have left the dog in the car and taken it? We have run into a couple of pretty rapid dog people up in Green Valley. Any chance it could have gotten out by itself? A couple lost their dog in The Dalles area some years ago and a dog psychologist said to keep looking in the area they lost it and that is where they finally found it. Of course that wouldn't apply if the dog couldn't get out. I'm just trying to look at this from a different angle since the reward approach has been fruitless. Good luck.

Post 97: Panchita - You have checked out the dog pound in Guaymas I assume?

Day 14 – March 14ᵗʰ
Post 98: Traveler - Mary has a good point about someone taking it upon themselves to "rescue" Lucky. Might want to whistle around the condos some morning.

Post 99: TheColoradoDude - Also check with the guard at Pilar. Peace, Love, & Fish Tacos!

Post 100: Jim - Good Morning! In regards to Mary's reply, I take pretty good care of Lucky and have done so for six years. He's my everyday companion at work in the office and when I cruise around. When I leave from anywhere, he has to be with me and it's just like that. Basically we start and end the day together. I have been blessed to provide very well for him as if he were my own kid. He's the celebrity in the office and at my desk. Lucky is well taken care of, and of course loved by many. Hence, the hard search.

A little more about this. Years ago I had Hodgkin's Disease, so as a result I can have no kids. The radiation scatter just made fertility almost impossible and proved itself over two marriages. So, over the years I've learned that (other than my nephews and nieces) "Man's Best Friend" is the most reliable source of day to day company and loyalty. Which is what I enjoy as a single person and Lucky was my choice when adopted here at six weeks.

Now about the car and someone else's perception of his safety that Saturday. I have felt a certain guilt about this. I've been thinking, "What if I did this or that," however, after deep personal review, I know that I left Lucky in the car safely as I always do. After all, I'm his keeper and basically "Dad." The only reason Lucky didn't join us on our walk was because the area was a protected wildlife sanctuary and the posted signs mentioned "No Dogs."

The temperature was fairly mild (around 72-73 at the water), the windows were down 3-4 inches (my trusting mistake), and the sunroof was completely open. The ocean breeze welcomed a comfortable walk through the estuary. The time was around 5:00 p.m. or so, which means the sun was hovering around the tops of the Pilar condos and surely the temperature was dropping. So you asked, "If my car was forcefully broken into?" Well, the person(s) involved reached through the slightly open rear window, unlocked the door, set off the alarm, stole a bottle of wine and a six pack of beer and other groceries. I believe the visual impact of my car being a Mercedes and their curiosity to look inside. I also believe the visual impact of the groceries started the motion.

When my alarm went off I was approximately 100 yards into the estuary and because of a heart condition I have, I couldn't run back, but walked at a fast pace. When I arrived, the door was closed, groceries gone and Lucky had also been taken with/by leash. I believe Lucky was thought of as an opportunity for reward and although I locked my car doors, I also believe I was not cautious enough about the windows. I've never had a bad experience out here.

However Mary, your comment stands in front of me making me think. Why have they not jumped on the $1,000.00 reward? I believe you're right, there may be something else behind this and I might be profiling kids and not thinking outside the box. So if that's the case, if there is anyone reading these posts who knows anything about Lucky and felt that I did something wrong please notify me privately and lets discuss this. I'm very sorry about the way you may feel; however, you have no idea the pain I'm going through right now, the work I'm sacrificing, the vacation I've lost and the lost sleep I've had. Thanks Jim

Post 101: Jim - Regarding the last post, and certainly what "Lucky" is going through. Jim

Post 102: RD - Jim, I don´t know you, but my heart goes out to you. I have never seen anyone make this kind of effort to find their dog and I sincerely hope your efforts are rewarded soon. Best of luck to you.

Post 103: Jim - Went to go see this pooch. He was funny, clever and retrieved a plastic chewed up cup. It was hard to leave as he wasn't Lucky. (attached photo of the dog).

Post 104: Jim - Another call and visit. Just not Lucky. I'm staying diligent in my hunt. (image posted)

Post 105: Jim – Lucky; No "Lucky" today. I drove around today with my eyes wide open, checking banners, managing Team Lucky and printing more flyers.

I also spent some time with Guaymas radio announcer Jorge Pompa from station 90.1 Radio Visa. Mr. Pompa and 90.1 has kindly donated air time over the last week with many spots during peak listening times of 4-6 p.m. Radio Visa is pulling the best out the Guaymas citizens. Similar to San Carlos, many Guaymas residents recognize Lucky now and the calls are coming in.

Mr. Pompa declared "Lucky" as the most famous dog in Sonora today and I'm counting on that. I'm praying for someone's heart to change. Good night, Jim.

Post 106: Repeat of Post 105

Post 107: Repeat of Post 105

Post 108: CDM - After reading post #100, I wonder when someone broke into the car if Lucky escaped. They may have chased him, but never caught him and he is still in the area. Team Lucky could get a group together to be in that area before sunrise until after sunset. Just a thought.

Post 109: SanCarlosMaverick - Team Lucky de Obregon distributed the flyers throughout the city, focusing on the local bus lines and local businesses. I'm convinced that whoever took Lucky was not concerned about his well-being, as they stole the groceries with wine and beer. It definitely was not a good Samaritan; but, rather a Mexican having the opportunity to gain access to the vehicle to steal the groceries and the dog. Once the local realizes that Lucky is neutered, Lucky's value is greatly reduced.

We distributed the flyers in the downtown area where the locals frequent and also at Sam's and Home Depot. I think Jesus already covered Walmart yesterday. Our maid and gardener also took flyers to give to the bus drivers and to distribute throughout the areas where they live. They were VERY excited at the generous reward amount. I also gave flyers to the guards at the various entrances to our community and asked them to work this weekend in their neighborhoods to see if anyone knows anything.

Although I think Lucky is alive and well in the Guaymas area, I am happy to help to be sure he hasn't been brought down to Obregon. The poor locals here are primarily interested in dogs for breeding purposes, while the well-to-do residents are more interested in puppies. I'm convinced that Lucky was stolen by a local Mexican with thoughts of breeding, but once that aspect is not an option, his primary value is as ransom.

I sincerely doubt that Lucky has been transported north of Hermosillo or south of Obregon. Please keep the pressure on in the Guaymas / Empalme area, because I think that's the greatest chance of success.

Don't EVER give up! Lucky will be returned. Mark

Post 110: Jim - Hi CDM and thanks for your post and thoughts. With regards to your thoughts, almost two weeks ago I saturated the Condo Pilar area. Including myself, we walked and sifted through the dry bed, mangroves, estuary path and Condo Pilar. Today, as a result of Mary's comment yesterday and the importance to pay attention to this, I placed a Team Lucky member outside Condo Pilar and asked him to scan the beach, enter the condos and distribute more flyers. He also walked and re-checked areas previously explored. Tomorrow, I'm going to sit back from a distance and develop a general profile over two days to see who visits this spot. Thanks, Jim Kawaguchi

Post 111: Lourdes - May God give you peace tonight as you sleep my sweet! ♥♡♡

Post 47.

Post 57.

Post 95.
(not Lucky)

Post 103.
(not Lucky)

Post 104.
(not Lucky)

6. Searching Beyond San Carlos and Guaymas

The reward had been upped to $1,000 U.S. dollars (or $13,000 Mexican pesos) and still, there was no true trace of my son. Yes, it felt like I was searching for my son; if Lucky were a human boy instead of a male dog, the only thing that would've gone differently is that, most likely, I would have been able to have had law enforcement heavily involved. In Mexico, it is not a high priority to investigate stolen or missing pets, whether they be dogs, cats or birds. Perhaps if a cow or horse is stolen, then a raised eyebrow and an investigation might occur.

I was now convinced by the Posting of others on Viva San Carlos that it was truly an act of treachery and downright thievery. A person who would steal another's pet, child, and or property is one of the lowest forms of life and should be slithering amongst the vipers in the high grass.

"What kind of animal would steal another animal?" I asked myself.

I was still blaming myself for the mix-up with the phone call from Hermosillo, going over and over and then over again on what I could have, should have, would have done differently. Had I been talking and texting with the thief that had stolen a big part of my heart—my Lucky? Was he at least a decent human being who would feed and water my best friend? *Oh, Lucky Boy, I am so sorry that I left you alone in the car that day just two weeks ago, that now seems like months*, I thought.

Everything had been great with my prior visits to San Carlos up until this point, and what a game-changer losing Lucky had been. I did not want to look at my home away from home, Mexico, differently, but how could I not. The pain was relentless and I could feel a bit of despise for the area arising from somewhere deep inside a hidden crevice of my soul. I did not want the regret of having moved to the Sonoran Desert next to the Sea of Cortez to flow into my blood; but, it was beginning to churn its way into my body. I needed to fight this with all my might and stay positive.

Lucky needed me to stay strong. I was the leader of his search party and he was depending on me to get him home safe. I had a task to complete; no time for bitterness to set in. I'd thank the Lord for the many blessings he had bestowed upon me and get a good night of sleep so that I might be rested and energized to march forward. Tomorrow was a new day and as long as there is life, there is hope.

2 Weeks - March 15th

Post 112: Caroline - Jim, did you contact directly all of the local vets both in San Carlos and Guaymas? There are quite a few and perhaps one of them might remember some-one bringing "Lucky" in to have him checked out for breed-ing. Since I have three wonderful dogs, who are like my family, your situation touches me deeply. May you have a miracle that brings your little boy back safe and sound. For me, this has been a painful lesson never to trust my dogs are safe unless they are inside my house and back yard. Everyone is praying and hoping for your miracle and will rejoice when we hear he is home safely. Caroline D.

Post 113: mmkatzz – I don't understand one thing, with all these calls and visits to see if these dogs are your Lucky, do all these people not know who their dog belongs to, or are they just on their street, or do they just want the money for their own dog? I am not getting why all these people come forward with all the adorable dogs for you to see, aren't they their dogs?

Post 114: Jim - Does anyone know exactly where the dog pound is next to the Guaymas airport?

Post 115: Jim - To mmkatz, Lucky has been receiving plenty of media attention. Combined with the street effort, posted banners, flyers and of course the reward amount, this is bound to happen. Lucky's information has been exposed to a weekly average of 10k people per week, with maybe 900 new per day. I'm getting all kinds of people calling and I'm grateful. Whatever the case, I'm checking every physical lead. One of them will be Lucky.

Post 116: mmkatzz - Thank you, and good luck.

Post 117: traveler – Roast: Mark, without really knowing the nationality of the perps it seems unfair to assign blame one way or the other.

Toast: Lots of people may develop a greater appreciation for their dogs, and dogs in general as demonstrated by Jim's efforts at recovering his friend and companion.

Post 118: SanCarlosMaverick - Traveler, as the only Gringo in the entire city of Obregon, I think I know the local community very well. My point was that if it was a good Samaritan who was "rescuing" Lucky, why steal all of the groceries as well. I was making a generalization, but probably a good one.

Anyhow, the Team Lucky de Obregon distributed ALL of the flyers yesterday and today. We hit the swap meets, local bus lines, veterinarians, pet groomers, banks, taco stands, fruit stands, newspaper sellers, policia, maids, street vendors, and just about every busy place we could find.

The high reward amount was greeted by MANY smiles from the locals. If Lucky is in Obregon, I'm confident he will be found, as the entire city has been covered. We even got offered a couple of white poodles that were someone's pet. Keep the faith Jim. Mark

Post 119: traveler - *Toast: For all your hard work Mark!*

Post 120: SanCarlosMaverick - You've got to love Team

Lucky de Obregon!

Sweet Olivia, my four year old is SO determined to find Lucky, she begged me to go out three times today with flyers. We hit all of the bus stops (taped the flyers to the posts and gave flyers to the drivers) and also hit Walmart (customers coming and going and also ALL of the workers in the parking lot). We even went to some places that we hadn't been to, but they showed us they already had Lucky's flyer. I'm firmly convinced that Ciudad Obregon is fully on alert. Congrats to Jim for his HUGE reward. That is what creates such an effort. We have had several locals ask for extra flyers so they can distribute them throughout their neighborhood. The majority of these locals work for less than 100 pesos per day, so $13,000 pesos to them is like hitting the lottery.

Little Olivia dressed up in her ballet outfit, so nobody could resist her when she approached them with the flyers. She speaks perfect Spanish and English, so she was able to translate perfectly. Mark and Olivia

March 16th

Post 121: Jim - Good Morning, get Everyeen days now and luck. (mistexted)

I want to give special thanks to Mark and his daughter for their outstanding effort in Obregon. Truly appreciated.

Today I plan to visit Mulipitas and take a look around. I've talked to them and they have flyers, but I haven't been to their facility. I'll also have my signs up and studying the visitors at the estuary again. Last, we'll be walking through the mud areas of the estuary again.

Time has gone by fast and no Lucky. Last night when I arrived home, I actually called out his name, waiting for him to come "ripping around the corner." Didn't happen. I ended up organizing my receipts from days' expenses, brushing my teeth. I'm hoping today will be the day!

Post 122: Jim - Last reply to start. Good morning everyone. Sixteen days and no Lucky.

Post 123: Sylvie - Early this morning, while driving to Extra on the back roads from the Ranchitos (main road being paved) I passed a white poodle boy trotting along. Called out 'Lucky" and he came to the car, but ran off when he saw my big boy in the passenger seat. Came back out, without my dog in 10 minutes, but couldn't find him. Did not see a red collar. Sylvie L.

Post 124: Jim – Sylvie, can you give me more info? Where is this and how do I get there? It will be my first search. Please let me know.

Post 125: Sylvie - Call me 226-xxxx. I drove from my house on Calle F and Third in Ranchitos to the back of Froggys before turning right to Extra. The poodle was trotting on the diverting paved road going to Guaymas. Sylvie L.

Post 126: Mary - From Beltrones, turn north at the Extra on the east end of town. You will drive by the Athletic Club. You can easily drive up and down the streets in Ranchitos from there.

Post 127: Sylvie - Call me, I'll meet you wherever.

Post 128: Sylvie - He ran off in the direction of Tony's Market. I'm going there now to check it out.

Post 129: Jim - Hi Sylvie, I just drove through the area and spoke with the gentleman working the market. Did not see. I put a Team Lucky member there "Armando," and he's looking around. Thanks Jim

Post 130: Jim - Hi Everyone. Just arrived home. Did my

rounds in Guaymas Norte. There are so many little developments. I did my slow drive through the neighborhoods and talked to many residents. I also spent time in the Ranchitos, Country Club, El Pilar and Los Jitos.

16 days now and no "Lucky." I'm still going to push on any ideas? Anything will continue to help.

Special thanks to: Mark, Mary, Sylvie, Panchita, Jon, Caroline. Your suggestions and help are appreciated.

I went to visit several dogs today including this one. He was lost and I was called to visit. If you know who may own him give me a buzz. I can help. Thanks and goodnight. Jim Kawaguchi (image attached)

March 17th, St. Patrick's Day

Post 131: Jim - Good morning. Doing my circle today and checking on "Lucky" banners. If anyone is going into La Manga, can you please check on the entrance banner (just after Puesta De Sol) and let me know if it's OK or needs some work.

Please continue your prayers for my little buddy. Thanks, Jim (attached image)

Post 132: SanCarlosMaverick - Jim, I admire your persistence and am confident that you will be reunited with your little buddy. I'm glad you chose to send me the flyers here in Obregon. The fact that it has been 17 days makes me think that maybe Lucky is not still in the Guaymas / San Carlos area. The large reward of $13,000 pesos should have been enough to have him returned by now.

Little Olivia is VERY determined to find Lucky. She insisted that we go out again yesterday to distribute the remaining flyers. We hit lots of local supermarkets, local eateries, and then the major outdoor market where they sell fish, meats, veggies, etc. Olivia is so cute, nobody could resist her handing out the flyers. I will be curious to see how many calls you get from her efforts. All it takes is THE ONE call and the return of Lucky.

Keep the faith. As Jim Valvano famously said, "Don't give up! Never give up!"

Mark and Olivia

Post 133: Jim - Thanks Mark!

Post 134: gbouschor - Many years ago when SBPA was still in its infancy in February, a Rottweiler was taken from the Beach at Pilar. The two fellows that owned the dog were in the water with their younger dog. The older Rottweiler was sitting on the beach and a pickup with family pulled up. The dog got in. SBPA was called, reward suggested, Posters, etc., all that we could do. Every call was responded to and every dog looked at. Believe it or not, there were dogs that didn't faintly resemble a Rottweiler. We spread the info to outlying areas. Late summer a call was received from someone who knew someone, who knew someone who saw the dog on a ranch somewhere between here and Ortiz. We had a woman who knew the area, paid her gas and off she went. Arriving she found the ranch abandoned, but someone said the people went to a ranch near Obregon. Off to Obregon she went. The dog was there. I will never understand how this "system" worked, but it did. He was recovered and brought back to San Carlos, the young men flew in from California and all were reunited. Lots of tears and smiles. It was October of that year before the dog was located. Miracles do happen, so don't give up hope. In Mexico so much gets "settled" by the passing of info, word of mouth. I wanted you to know all things are possible and sometimes we must wait longer than we like, just keep the flame of hope alive and the search ongoing. We are all keeping our eyes out for him. Gwen B

Post 135: Maggy - I was at the old Soriana a couple of days ago and someone put a very nice Postcard on my windshield about "Lucky." Don't lose hope, he will be found!

Post 136: Jim - Lucky; I know the effort is working. Every time I'm called out, the little guys look closer and closer to Lucky. The communities are really becoming familiar with what to look for. Jim (attached image)

Post 137: TropicalGirl - I'm confused, some comments are from 2008 and some from 2011. When did Lucky go missing and has he been found?

Post 138: PT - LOL, that's funny, something wrong with the current dates here. Maybe the moderator has to adjust that. Lucky got lost a bit over two weeks ago.

Post 139: Marlinmaster - T.G., I think you are looking at people's register dates, not Post dates. (Author's note: Marlinmaster was correct)

March 18th

Post 140: Jim - Good Morning, I didn't find Lucky yesterday. I searched the Los Jitos / Golf Course area, drove through Central Guaymas and am considering a billboard as a fixed, long-term ad for Lucky. If there is anyone that owns one, or can refer me to a company, that would be appreciated. Will be working central Guaymas today. If there are any suggestions, please let me know.

Special thanks to Gwen, Maggy, Mark and Audean for her special phone call. Off to another day. Today may be the day! Jim

Post 141: Gatita - Vaya con Dios.

Post 142: mach1 - Been following this so closely and wishing and hoping for the best every day. Your dedication and love for "Lucky" is an inspiration. Can't say as I blame you, he is an image of my little "Tom" who is one the brightest spots in my life. I'm so sorry you're going through this and so sorry if Lucky is feeling lost and alone. Please don't give up. Your dedication will pay off, I know it. Someone has him. There are people out there who know where he is. It's just a matter of time. My very best wishes for success, for you and for Lucky. Donna C.

March 19th

Post 143: Jim - Good Morning. No "Lucky" yesterday, but had a chance to meet more people from the outlying areas. I am receiving responses from Obregon, (Thanks Maverick) and took a look at one pooch who was very similar to Lucky, but just wasn't him.

Team Lucky will be in San Carlos today with their hand held banners. If you see them, please wave or honk and show your support.

I'll be meeting with a local businessman to discuss long-term commercial highway signage for Lucky. As I eventually have to leave (week or so), and go home to other responsibilities, I thought this might be a way to keep Lucky in front of everyone. If anyone has any other ideas, please let me know. Also, I'm going to get in a hard work out today to help relax my body and mind. I haven't done this since Lucky disappeared.

I would like to acknowledge the following people for their recent support: Jon, Mark, Gatita, Gwen and Donna. Please, keep your support coming. If anyone would like to help with the following that would be appreciated: Research for Groomers, Vets, Rescue and Dog Pounds in both Obregon and Hermosillo. In identifying these different groups, in those cities and creating a mailing and phone list for me to contact. If I could get a little help from anyone, it can really help bring Lucky home. Thanks! Jim

Post 144: Mary - You have been Posting a lot of pictures of dogs that aren't Lucky. It might be good to rePost a picture of the real thing, with as many vital statistics as possible.

Post 145: Jim - In reply to Mary;

Lucky:

1. Poodle mix; White with very, very light brown hairs around shoulder.
2. 12-14 lbs
3. Red and green Christmas collar
4. Identification tags with his and my name and number
5. Chip installed (Home Again)
6. Hair is probably long and maybe matted at this time with light hints of "blue color" due to a mohawk located on top of head. Much longer hair in center of head than the sides if Lucky has not been groomed at this point.
7. Two missing teeth on lower, center jaw
8. Will sing with you
9. Stands 14-16 inches high

I hope this helps.

Post 146: WyYnot - Jim, I have a dad doing a little work for me today that lives in Guaymas. When he has no construction work he raises plants and then drives up and down the streets here in Guaymas and in Empalme. He works with his two teenage sons and he is very trustworthy. I have known him for nearing ten years. They take care of our little place and dogs when we need to trip up North. They have dogs of their own in Guaymas and love our dogs as well. I could visit with him on handing out little flyers and photos in his travels, selling from his little pickup. Maybe stick on a megaphone similar to El Vigia with a short message about Lucky, LOL. Let me know if you have some extra flyers / pictures. They actually think they may have seen Lucky about a week ago, over near Ruth and Rudy's at Los Arcos. Ron

Post 147: Jim - Good evening or good morning. No Lucky

today. Received a few calls, but, not a match. Today, Lucky was blessed by a local businessman who donated a commercial sign located at entrance of San Carlos. I think it's a nice location and will give my little buddy further exposure. If you were driving around San Carlos today you should have seen a few "Team Lucky" members holding up signs. Tomorrow could be the day! (attached image)

March 20th

Post 148: Jim - Lucky; Jorge Pompa, disc jockey for RadioVisa 90.1 has donated airtime over the last two weeks and now is helping our search in Obregon. Soon Lucky will be on the airways there. Moving part of our team there tomorrow.

I know we are doing our best! (photo attached of Jorge Pompa and Jim in the studio)

Post 149: Repeat of Post 148

Post 150: Sheilasu – Jim, it breaks my heart to read your messages about sweet Lucky. I hope that his name is a God-send, and that he will be lucky and get home to you - SOON. I saw one of your people, Armando? Near the corner by Santa Rosa today, and spoke with him. I have been looking for Lucky everywhere I go, without luck.

I want to thank you for all of the information; I often leave my little mini Dachshund, Maximo Valentino in my car with the windows down a few inches and the sunroof open, I won't be doing that in the future. God Bless and I pray that Lucky gets home to you quickly. Sheila

March 21st

Post 151: Jim - Good Morning! Moving Team Lucky to Guaymas today and then planning Obregon. I didn't visit any pooches yesterday, but there is this little poodle mix that keeps showing up at Los Jitos. I'm going to stay there for awhile today and see for myself.

Today could be my "Lucky" day! Persistence! Jim

Post 152: Jim - I'm working hard now as we enter Obregon. I have covered San Carlos and the search started developing in Obregon. Today Lucky was blessed with talk radio 105 FM in Guaymas. This radio station reaches Obregon, and I believe the airtime was perfect as Team Lucky will be there tomorrow. I have two members that will be working the central populated area with banners and flyers.

Thank you radio host: Paulina Acosta Velasco! Obregon will be a hard push. (photo image of DJ Paulina Acosta Velasco)

Post 153: SanCarlosMaverick - Jim, please PM me with the locations that your team members plan on setting up. As I live here, I can make suggestions and also assist in the effort. Mark

Post 154: Jim - Hi Mark! Will do. Leaving San Carlos and then stopping in Guaymas for half an hour. I'll PM you when I leave and get us organized! Thanks so much. Jim

Post 130.
(not Lucky)

Post 131.
(Jim posted another picture of Lucky with his mohawk)

Post 136.
(not Lucky)

Post 147.
(Billboard frame donated for Lucky)

Post 148. Jorge Pompa, Disc Jockey for RadioVisa 90.1 & Jim.

Post 152. Radio Host Paulina Acosta Velasco.

7. Realization of Life Without Lucky

It had been over three weeks since my best friend was taken and more than two days since I'd posted anything about Lucky, or of the ever-ongoing search that took over all my thoughts, all my strength, all my being.

The roughest of Obregón helped in tampering my enthusiasm for finding my son. Obregón was not the town that I thought it to be, or what I had envisioned in my thoughts. For some reason I had expected it to be similar to Guaymas. I knew it had less persons living there, but, had no idea to the extent of the road conditions with its sharp turns that prevented anyone from seeing any oncoming traffic before, during, or after, until it was too late. There are lots of pedestrians there that choose to not look both ways, and police officers who await for my inexperience of driving in such horrific conditions.

My friend Mark makes his home in Obregón and went out of his way to try and make me feel at home and as comfortable as possible during my street gleaning and talking with the residents of his town. On a positive note, many of the local townspeople had already heard of Lucky and there had been many responses of up and down shakes of the head and, "*Sí. Sí, Lucky el perro que perdido.*" English translation: "Yes. Yes, Lucky the dog that is lost."

I became even more exhausted and felt as if I were the one that was lost.

March 23rd–

Post 155: Gatita - Any new leads? We're all still with you and little Lucky. Buena suerte hoy! Translation - (Good Luck today)

Post 156: SanCarlosMaverick - My wife just got a photo of Lucky's flyer sent to her cell phone by a friend. Apparently someone was handing out flyers today in Obregon. Her friend remarked that it was the same flyer my wife had Posted to her Facebook. In addition, my wife has already sent photos of the flyer to all of her friends in Obregon, Hermosillo, and Navajoa. The search network is expanding, so let's hope and pray for Lucky's safe return.

I'm out of flyers, but, if someone is still in Obregon with flyers I would suggest they tape several to the red Posts by the bus stop on the east side of the Walmart parking lot (main street side). Olivia and I taped at least half a dozen there and I noticed on Friday that all of them were missing. That's a prime local bus stop and Olivia and I also gave several to the bus drivers when they stopped. I don't think the flyers were taken down and thrown away, because several other flyers were still in place when we checked. That huge reward likely caused bus users to take a flyer with them when they got on the bus. Olivia and I had several bus riders ask for extra flyers to distribute in their neighborhoods. Keep up the determined effort. More and more people are hearing about Lucky's disappearance. Mark

Post 157: Mary - Last year my friend's car was broken into at the Estero parking lot next to Pilar. They stole purses. 30 minutes later they used her credit card at the Pemex at El Valiente. In other words, they fled immediately and headed north. Have you hit that area hard? Have you Posted on the online sites in the US for lost dogs and looked at the found ones? The supposition with my friend is that a guy on a bicycle broke into their car and then headed into the dune area next to Condos Delfines and hooked up with a truck or car. If your dog was dumped there and picked up by an RV (they camp around there) who then headed north, it's possible they would have not heard about the theft, but might have Posted online. Just a thought as everything is grasping at straws at this point.

Post 158: Jim - Good Evening everyone,

To start, I apologize about not Posting over the last two days. I know there are many followers and I'm accountable during or at the end of the day; however, just recently I've been very tired.

I have found out over the last two days that Obregon is much worse (to me) than driving through the streets of New York City. The drivers and roadways are the worst I've maneuvered through yet. Lots of traffic, blind turns, jaywalkers and defensive driving. To make it worse and note my driving skills in this town, I was pulled over three times by local traffic police. If it wasn't for Letty, I would have been ticketed all three times. Fortunately, the cost was only 50 pesos. The officers were polite and understanding. While working my way through each situation, I showed the flyer's of Lucky. Two of them recognized Lucky and mentioned seeing the banners and previous flyers of him. With that said, I have to give many thanks and kudos to Maverick Mark, as it was most likely his starting effort that made Obregon aware of my little buddy and interested. So, thanks Mark!

Today, before I left, I spent much time with Jon Hildebrand in his office. For the first time in a long time I was able to relax and chat with him and his wife, Jen. Our time together was spent discussing Lucky and the possibility of looking into Hermosillo. I did discuss this with Gwen and Caroline as well. As a result, I do think it's a great idea, and I'm going to start laying out my research tomorrow with groomers and Vets. Then I'll move a majority of my effort there and make a huge push over the next week with flyers and new banners.

I have a neighbor here who owns Azteca television in Hermosillo and I'm praying that he offers a small broadcasted story about Lucky as I enter. Before I leave, I'll be contacting local radio as I did in Guaymas.

To me, this ordeal has been and continues to be surreal. I do believe I'm running on adrenaline and shock right now. As I'm now mentally and physically tired, I do realize sooner or later that I'm going to have to leave this effort. The safety and return will be bequeathed in GOD's hands.

For the last two weeks, Lucky will have my full attention, full spirit and hard work until the beginning of April. It's then, that I'll have to pass the baton to GOD and/or someone else. Then I have to leave.

With intent, I do believe I'll be here in San Carlos during Semana Santa (Easter Week) to reach a crowd of young people that ideally match my search demographics. I feel that cross marketing Lucky's information to one lump of people that may represent up to four separate cities at once will maximize everyone's efforts and gain the best exposure for Lucky. By doing this, I believe expenditures will be reduced and we all might see Lucky sooner. That's if Lucky is not revealed in Obregon or Hermosillo. I should reach perhaps three to five thousand young adults.

Again, many thanks to Mark, Caroline, Gwen, Jon and Jen. Your kind help is appreciated.

Tonight, I had a drink, Crown Royal Reserve and Coke, and boy it was a nice evening cap. So, if you should find anything out of order such as punctuation or writings, please forgive me as it's the exhaustion and spirits working away at me. Good Night. Jim

March 24th

Post 159: Jim - Mark would you like me to send more? I really need to hit all the vets and groomers there.

Post 160: SanCarlosMaverick - Jim, your comments regarding driving in Obregon gave me a good chuckle. We avoid driving in the Centro on weekends because it's so crazy and driving is hazardous. You really have to apply your defensive driving skills. It's a miracle that we've never been pulled over or involved in an accident. I'm not surprised that many people were already aware of Lucky's flyer. Little Olivia made sure we gave one to every policia that we saw, as well as bus drivers, vets, and groomers.

Yes, please send some more flyers. We can continue the search efforts here in Obregon. Many people here in Obregon also have family members living in other parts of Mexico, so the word will spread to other areas as well. When we ran out of flyers I had to tell Olivia that Lucky was found, so she would stop worrying about him and insisting we go out looking for him. Saturday we went to Walmart and several of the parking lot attendants asked us if Lucky was found, so I finally had to tell her that the dog that looked like Lucky turned out to be the wrong dog. We will keep up the efforts here until Lucky is safely back in your lap.

I think we now need to look at this search as a marathon, rather than a sprint. Usually quick action is the best option for achieving a successful return of the dog. Your large reward will be a key factor is his return. I don't know anyone here in Mexico that would keep the dog in lieu of the reward, especially given Lucky's age and being neutered. People go CRAZY over my female, white golden retriever and I quickly tell them that she is 10 years old and is spayed, because I have found that the next question out of their mouths is usually, "How many puppies has she had?"

Let me know when you send the flyers so Olivia and I can continue the search efforts throughout Obregon. Mark

Post 161: Jim - Hi everyone. No Lucky today. There were three calls from Guaymas and one from Obregon.

The call in Obregon was investigated. Maverick Mark, his daughter and wife were very generous and kind to go visit the property and speak with the home owner. As it turns out, it just wasn't Lucky.

Tomorrow, I'll be meeting with Carlos the "sign" guy to take care of business. I hope this is up by Saturday.

Today I didn't get pulled over anywhere.

Again, many thanks for all your prayers and again, Mark and his family in Obregon. You are a Godsend!

March 25th

Post 162: Jim - Good morning.

Today I'm planning to meet the billboard guy, plan another visit to Obregon and send Mark more flyers. Team Lucky will be at the entrance and exit of San Carlos. Lastly, I am planning to go into Hermosillo.

Please if there are any people, support or ideas that you may have, or can suggest in Hermosillo to help find Lucky please let me know!! Thanks your help is needed. Jim

Post 163: SanCarlosMaverick - Yes, we had an exciting day yesterday. Jim got a call from a woman who had one of Lucky's flyers and noticed that her neighbor had a new dog that closely resembled Lucky. At first the only information we had was a street address (unfortunately, there was some misunderstanding because the street name given did not exist). Finally, close to 5:30 p.m. Jim got the correct street name and address. I was able to locate the house on Google earth and Olivia and I jumped in the car and raced over to the house while there was still a little daylight. The house was located in one of the barrios in the far southwest of the city, so it's not an area one would want to venture after dark. We got to the house and discovered that the dog looked like Lucky, but turned out to be a young (one year old) female. They offered us the dog in exchange for the reward, but we passed.

The good news is that so many people are now aware of Lucky's disappearance that they are paying attention to new dogs in their neighborhoods that resemble Lucky. That was the case yesterday where the neighbor said that this dog arrived at the house over the weekend. Turns out it was brought down from Hermosillo.

Maybe the next call will be THE call. That faith is what

keeps us going.

Jim is sending more flyers, so Olivia and I will hit the streets once again. They are in the process of constructing the 4th phase of our housing development, so distributing the flyers to all of the workers is a great way to get the word out, as the workers live throughout the entire city. We also have targeted the trash guys, water distributors, Telmex installers, etc., as they travel to all parts of the city in their daily work duties. Mark and Olivia

Post 164: Jim - Hi Mark, I just sent the flyers via Tufesa. Will pm you with details. Thanks!

Post 165: Amigo2 - You might go to the pet stores and groomers in Hermosillo. Several years ago our white Bishon was stolen from us here in San Carlos and after a month of intense searching, he was located in Hermosillo. A local groomer had worked on him and remembered who brought him in. Steve H.

Post 166: Porsche - Today when the border patrol asked for my dog's shot and health records going into Arizona, I gladly presented them.

I asked if it was because they were looking for Lucky. The Officer did not know anything about the white poodle. Would it help to advise our border guards?

Post 167: SanCarlosMaverick - The last two Posts are excellent suggestions. I think we are reaching the point of "leave no stone unturned." My wife's brother works and lives in Hermosillo and comes back to Obregon on the weekends. This weekend I will give him flyers and ask him to distribute them to the vets and groomers in Hermosillo. As for the border agents, maybe someone like Casa Imports that makes frequent trips would be willing to give them a few flyers on their next few crossings.

Little Olivia had a good idea also. She suggested we go to the Obregon bus terminal and hand out flyers to the passengers and families traveling throughout Mexico. It's an extremely busy bus terminal and has destinations throughout the country. She and I will do that throughout the next couple of weeks.

Mark and Olivia, Team Lucky de Obregon

March 27th

Post 168: Caroline - Any updates on "Lucky?" We are all hoping to get some good news soon!

Post 169: Jim - Good evening. Today was not quite a "Lucky" day, but was productive. I continued with Armando passing out flyers with Betty later holding Lucky's banner in Obregon. Mark and Olivia passed out flyers too.

Yesterday I gathered up information on vets and groomers in Hermosillo as suggested by Amigo and others. Today, Letty, Lupita, Carmen and I visited 16 of the 30 listed. They all have Lucky's information and will keep it quiet until or if that "special visit" arrives.

Hermosillo compared to Obregon is a much easier and safer town to work in. However the long, dark drive home is dangerous. You really have to be alert.

I did receive multiple calls and pictures from Obregon, San Carlos and Hermosillo.

Next week unfortunately, I have to start planning my leave for three weeks. If there is anyone that would like to join Letty, please let me know. We could really use extra people to help or donate a few hours. (If Lucky is not home yet.)

Thanks for all your advice. Every little bit has helped. Good night, Jim

Post 170: T Bird Richard - Suggestion from the "for what it's worth department." Why not expand the search a little further South to Navojoa? Spread Lucky's picture(s) among the listed vets and see if any have treated him for anything. Navojoa vets get a lot of Alamos patients and who knows? Maybe, just maybe, we could get "Lucky". Richard B.

March 28th

Post 171: SanCarlosMaverick - Update from Team Obregon de Lucky:

Jim sent more flyers, so Olivia and I hit the main bus station where people are traveling to all parts of Mexico. We gave a flyer to every single passenger. We also gave a flyer to each of the vendors (magazines, food, snacks, etc.) inside the bus station. Then we went outside and gave flyers to each of the taxi drivers, local bus drivers, and every single business across from the station. Most of the businesses immediately taped the flyer to their front window for all to see. We distributed at least 100 flyers. Those flyers should reach a multitude of cities, many of which haven't been personally contacted.

Then we went to every veterinarian and groomer in the city. We were received well and all flyers were taped to the windows next to the entrance.

Today we will return to Walmart and tape numerous flyers on the Posts by the big bus stop, as well as hand out flyers to customers. I'll also make sure all of the parking lot attendants still have a flyer from our prior visits.

We'll use the remaining flyers over the weekend when we will return to the main bus terminal to distribute them to the waiting passengers. I think total saturation is the key, especially given the length of time Lucky has been missing. I personally don't think Lucky is still in the GSC area, as someone surely would have opted for the large reward by now. Lucky could be in Hermosillo, Obregon, Navajoa, or another city within Mexico (hopefully not already having crossed NOB). Having access to the bus passengers going to these other cities is a great opportunity to spread the word. Suerte, (Luck) Mark and Olivia

Post 172: DaveP - I think Mr. Lucky is either in Guaymas or Hermosillo.

More dogs that Jim
went to see, none
were Lucky.

Seems like there are so many dogs that closely resemble Lucky.

8. Hermosillo, Here We Come!

Just a couple of days ago we expanded our search into the largest city which is also the capital city of the State of Sonora–Hermosillo. I was overwhelmed by the magnitude of this sprawling city. While laying out our strategy of areas to cover, had to do quite extensive research on the area of which I found interesting and mind boggling.

Hermosillo's economic role in modern history was established in 1881 with the railroad connection to the port of Guaymas on the Sea of Cortez, and to the border city of Nogales, Arizona about four hours north of Hermosillo. The railroad opened both Mexican and U.S. markets to Sonora's mineral and agricultural products. The region maintains a strong agriculture and ranching industry with a population of three-quarters of a million people. Yes you read that correctly, home to 750,000 Hermosillians. The City of Hermosillo itself is home to both light and heavy industrial development and is considered the center for commerce in the State of Sonora. It also is Sonora's academic and research center, home to several universities, which gives it a high percentage of educated blue-collar and white-collar workers.

While working the Hermosillo area, I called it the town of never-ending roads. But, with such a vast outlay of land covering 7,745 miles, I also saw opportunity to find our Lucky. No longer did Lucky just belong to me, he now belonged to the Sonoran people of San Carlos, Guaymas, Empalme, Obregón and now Hermosillo, and all the little villages in between, as pretty much the entire state was helping in the search to find the bad person (or persons) who stole Lucky and the prize of Lucky himself. Lucky was now the wonder dog of Sonora.

I believe it was on our first trip to Hermosillo on March 27th, after a late lunch and a day of organizing our work in Hermosillo that Lupita (who is Alvaro L.'s wife, Carmen L., and Letty A.) had joined the mariachis that were playing at the restaurant by giving a cheer, "Go Lucky." It was a nice, uplifting way to end the workday.

I continued to find the strength and willingness to find my buddy.

March 29th

Post 173: Jim - Hi everyone, No Lucky yet. Spent yesterday in Hermosillo passing out more flyers. The population is so high that I'm not sure how to cover it correctly. I've been through the Costco / Mega market parking lots and a near street corner.

Yesterday, we went through 700 flyers just there. Can anyone suggest how this large town should be approached? Guaymas and the other towns took time; but, I and Team Lucky covered it well. Hermosillo is like staring at an endless road.

I've worked the groomers and vets as well.

Any suggestions or contacts there that anyone can offer? Thanks, Jim

Post 174: GeorgeInSanCarlos - Suggest you find the public bus terminal/s and get the drivers to Post the fliers in their buses. A few pesos and a few rolls of tape would be a good idea.

Post 175: Jim - Will do George! Thanks!

March 30th

Post 176: Jim - Good morning. Received a strong lead from a veterinarian last night. They do believe Lucky was there two weeks ago and they are creating a list of all poodles/mixes seen. They can't recall the family name, but by the description, age, and teeth, they say he's a match.

Monday, I'll be out there again, going through the list and visiting each household. Thanks for your support. Jim

Post 177: Mary - Good news. What city are you talking about?

Post 178: Jim - Hermosillo! This seems to be a strong lead.

Post 179: SanCarlosMaverick - That's VERY encouraging news Jim! Especially getting the call from a veterinarian who would have noticed the missing bottom front teeth and him being neutered. Hopefully the vet keeps detailed records (name, address, phone number, etc.) of the people that bring in their animals for treatment.

There are several different scenarios on how Lucky ended up in Hermosillo. We don't know if the original target was Lucky and/or the groceries (beer, wine, food). It's possible that whoever has Lucky is not aware of the theft. However, it is also possible that these are the "bad guys," as little Olivia refers to them, or friends or relatives of the bad guys.

My wife and Olivia are having lunch right now with her brother who lives in Hermosillo. If you find out that Lucky is in a bad neighborhood, he is willing to go with you. He plays defensive tackle for Itson's American football team, so he has an imposing physical presence. Although, if you pinpoint Lucky's location you may want to contact the local policia to be sure things go smoothly. Who knows what the situation will be? I know that when Olivia and I followed up on the lead you had in Obregon, it turned out to be in a bad area. It was a little unnerving knocking on the front door and having some of the neighbors gathering around to see what the heck the "Gringo" was doing in their hood. I wouldn't have taken Olivia with me if I had known ahead of time where the house was located. However, with only 30 minutes of daylight remaining I had to proceed. Hopefully, whoever has Lucky, found him or he was given to them innocently by someone who found him.

Please let everyone know of your progress. We hope and

pray Lucky will be back safely on your lap, singing away.

Mark and Olivia, Team Lucky de Obregon

March 31st

Post 180: Jim - Good Morning!

Well, I'm with prayer that today I'll be back with Lucky. As mentioned in a previous Post, Mark, I'm on my way to Hermosillo to visit with a vet who will be submitting some client information for me to review and visit. Today, I will be traveling with Letty and Lupita who both know the area well. I should arrive by 11, be with the vet at 12 and then off hunting by 1 p.m. As I progress, I'll try to Post.

Thanks to Mark and everyone's support. Jim

Post 181: Guzzi - Good luck.

Post 182: PT - 😊😊😊 I have a feeling, that this could be a great day for you Jim!

Post 183: mach1 - You've got a fan club in this house (3 people + 12 animals) all pulling for you. Good luck.

Please let us know how you make out. Donna, Moe, & Christine et al. Donna C.

Post 184: Jules - Please God, let this be the day Lucky comes home! Jules

Post 185: Caroline - Sending all the positive energy and prayers I can to help this be the day to bring your boy home.

Post 186: Starfish - Sending prayers for a joyful reunion!

April 1st

Post 187: Jim - Dear Friends, Today was a productive and positive day. After our visit with a Veterinarian, Lucky was again positively identified. Description of Lucky was perfect.

From the frazzled Mohawk, the missing bottom two teeth, being neutered to temperament.

They were kind enough to stick their necks out by disclosing a few leads. Thereafter, we made the phone calls and spoke to all of them except one. From our research, there were 13 poodle mixes brought in to this vet throughout the month of March.

So, we left with our information and started "cold calling" the list. To most they were receptive and to a few they were ordinarily concerned about the random phone call and their information. Out of these, there are three dogs that are of great interest. I need to aggressively locate one named "Troy." There is one problem, I don't have addresses and only phone numbers. I'm hoping that I have forged enough relationships to help with this dilemma. (If anyone can help, please PM me).

Tomorrow, although I submitted a verbal and hand written report in here and in Guaymas, I'll be filling out a written "formal" police report here to be documented throughout Mexico's database. A copy of this report needs to be given to this veterinarian and others. Additionally, for more secure recovery, a copy of "Home Again" embedded chip documents. Both reports will tie Lucky directly to me, legally and halt any struggle.

With the above information, and knowing Lucky is perhaps with a person who may care for him, I'm trying to decide, "Do I wait until Lucky comes back to the groomer/vet and stay low, knowing he is safe and not to scare them off," or "do I aggressively put pressure on the vets surrounding the community and lure someone out for the reward?"

I'm not sure really how to handle this. With the confidant that came forward, I do believe this is it. I believe I've located Lucky and whatever choice I make is critical to his proper return. I know "Lucky" has developed much interest throughout San Carlos and I know most of you have developed your thoughts.

Please, this is an important time to express them! Sincerely, Jim

Post 188: GeorgeInSanCarlos - I think, as a general rule, that people will take their dog to the Vet nearest their home. I would be papering the neighborhood, the schools and the bus stops. Let your offered reward work for you.

Post 189: Porsche – Don't wait. If the vet has their phone number, he could say he wants to check something, he is watching on the dog and to bring him in for free.

Suggestion number two: If you have the address, take a local priest with you and money. I would move quickly because if these people are innocent, someone else who reads Viva board could steal the dog and here we go again.

Post 190: SanCarlosMaverick - First of all, great news that you know Lucky is safe and the general area where he is! As for a suggestion for which next step to take, that's a difficult one. I don't think it would be wise to ask the vet to call the person and try to trick them into coming back to his office. That would really put the vet in a bad position, which could result in some sort of retribution to him or his property. I think the vet has already stuck his neck out enough by helping you to the extent he has.

My first inclination is similar to George's, which would be to saturate the surrounding neighborhoods with Lucky's flyers. However, that could also scare the family that has Lucky into relocating him with a friend or relative in another area if they have become attached to him in these past few weeks.

Hopefully you were able to gauge the family's disposition when you spoke to them on the phone. I think it's wise to file the proper police reports, etc. to be sure you don't get into any legal problems. After all, YOU are the visitor to this country.

I'll talk with my wife this afternoon and then we can discuss it further. Being born and raised here, she knows how the locals think. In the meantime, pray for guidance. Mark

Post 191: PobreBurro - I check every day for a new thread with the heading, "WE HAVE LUCKY!" Best of luck. I like the local Priest idea, if it could be worked out.

Post 192: Goldin - I would thread lightly at this junction and consider all your safe options. If the neighborhood where Lucky is, hears about the reward, you may start the cycle all over again, with neighbors trying to kidnap him for the money, with who knows what consequences.

Have you considered talking to the local police with all your documents and asking for help with the phone company? Maybe with the phone number you have and the police presence, the phone company may relinquish the name/address of Lucky's keepers. Then, the police with you, you can go to the home to get Lucky back. Good luck.

Post 193: SanCarlosMaverick - Jim, call me and give me the phone number. I have some connections that may be able to provide the address. Then you can decide whether to bring the policia or priest or whomever with you to get Lucky back. Mark

Post 194: Ja – Jim, if you know someone who is a good friend with a Telmex person, for a few bucks you can get an address from that phone number, Ja.

I have done this many times in life, Canada, USA and here in Mexico. Money for an address. The police can do it too, BUT, they won't want to; it's not a big crime case. LOL, and once in 1975 in Chile looking for a worker.

9 ❧ April Showers of Tears

I became quite discouraged after believing we were so very close to getting Lucky back. I was completely confused as to what was taking place with Lucky and the motivation or thinking of the person (or persons) who'd stolen my loved one. I was almost sure that the dog referred to as "Troy" was Lucky. The description from the veterinarian was exact: a white poodle mix with the frazzled mohawk, he was missing his two bottom teeth, his being neutered, and the temperament witnessed by the animal doctor. It had been all positive and a complete match.

My thinking is that he was named "Troy" because of mohawk-style haircut coincides with Trojan helmets worn during the time of Helen of Troy. The Trojan War was waged against the city of Troy by the Achaeans (Greeks) after Paris of Troy took Helen from her husband Menelaus, King of Sparta. The war is one of the most important events in Greek mythology and has been narrated through many works of Greek literature, most notably through Homer's *Iliad.* This may be one crazy theory, but it is what first entered into my mind as to why the dog had been given such a non-Mexican or Spanish name.

I feared that Lucky had been moved, perhaps sold for a small fraction of the reward and was now with new people because of the fear caused after seeing us canvas the area, or seeing the freshly printed and handed-out flyers in his or her neighborhood; perhaps they did not want to take a chance on someone calling in for the reward. Many different scenarios were playing in my head and my heart had given in to sorrow and negativity towards Mexico and San Carlos. I gave my land trust to a local realtor to look over and strongly considered putting my house in Bahia Esmeralda in San Carlos on the market. Never again to return to the area. My work responsibilities could no longer be ignored and I needed to return back to Temecula, CA if I was to salvage what business I had lost due to neglect as I'd given my full attention and focus to bringing Lucky back home.

I had not yet given up completely and was still following through on putting up a billboard sign similar to the flyers we had been handing out showcasing the now $26,000 peso reward without investigation or questions.

As I thought more and more about the possibility of never being reunited with my son, for some reason I began thinking about many of the past dogs in my life. I do believe that I was thinking about my babies that had all left this world due to cancer or old age because my mind and brain were trying to soften the blow to my heart by putting Lucky in the same category of having moved on. Perhaps I was preparing myself for the worst of news–that of no news nor of closure.

I needed to remind myself of all the blessings that had been given to me in the past and of the many hardships and illnesses that my dear Lord GOD had bestowed upon me. My mind drifted back.

April 4th

Post 196: SanCarlosMaverick - Jim, please provide an update on your search for Lucky. So many of us are anxious to hear some news, especially after your Post Monday that you were confident that Lucky was in Hermosillo and was seen by a vet recently. Olivia asks me EVERY morning if Lucky is back with Jim. So far I have only been able to tell her that you are getting closer every day. Thanks, Mark

Post 197: SanCarlosMaverick - I just spoke with Jim's Team Lucky in San Carlos and the reason we haven't gotten any of Jim's updates is that he had to go on a scheduled trip to California and will be returning to San Carlos shortly after Easter. Jim's team is handing out flyers in the neighborhoods surrounding the vet's office. I asked for the phone number so that I can try to get the name and address of the person they suspect has Lucky.

I'm sure Jim will update us when he returns. Until then, keep sending prayers for Lucky's safe return. Mark and Olivia - Team Lucky de Obregon

April 10th

Post 198: Jim - Hi everyone, I just wanted to say I'm back in California and getting back on track here. However, my work for "Lucky" has not stopped. I'm in contact with a friend in Hermosillo who is going to fine tune my research there and also finishing up my billboard design for the San Carlos entrance. This should be completed shortly. Calls are still coming in, but they are not matching Lucky. Being home here is very quiet. I still believe he's under my desk at times or resting at my feet while watching a ball game. I'm still trying to adapt for the time being. I do believe it's just a matter of time. Good night, Jim

Post 199: Goldin - Hello Jim, can you pick up where you left off after your Post #187. We thought you had found Lucky from your last contact with the Hermosillo vet. What happened?

April 17th

Post 200: Jim - Lucky is still loved and missed. The billboard sign will be up today at the far entrance into San Carlos, almost directly across from Delfinario. With the high influx of people coming in, this should be great exposure. We are still working Hermosillo. (attached image)

Post 200.

"Lucky's" billboard.

Everyone is trying to cash in on the $26,000 peso reward, even if it meant selling their own pet.

10. Lucky or Not Lucky? That is the Question!

I finally came to the realization and tried to slowly warn my heart that Lucky was not coming back. I only hoped and prayed that whoever took my little amigo was caring for him and had given him a loving home with lots of attention, water and doggie treats.

I decided that I would adopt a new friend and I would go the local humane society tomorrow. My thinking was that I needed another friend and there are dogs out there, that too need friends. With mixed emotions of extreme sadness from losing a lost, loved one and excited giddiness of possibly gaining a new friend for life, I pulled back the covers of my bed, laid my head on my pillow, wiped the tears from my face with the sleeve of my pajama top, and closed my eyes. I asked God to help me through this ordeal.

I awoke on the morning of May 8th with soft sadness in my heart, but with a slight smile on my face. Today was a new beginning and the coffee tasted extra good that morning. I was going to go to the shelter and was sure a new friend would pick me, instead of me being the chooser.

While on my drive to Thousand Oaks to Shelter Hope Pet Shop, thousands of memories of Lucky are enveloping me. I had chosen the Shelter Hope Pet Shop because of their good work and of their motto: "Dedicated to connecting pets and people." Shelter Hope Pet Shop was created to aid shelter pet adoptions, promote education and bring awareness to the communities they serve. It was the first volunteer humane pet shop that partnered with companies, such as NewMark Merrill and that donated storefront space in busy shopping locations in order to assist with community outreach and shelter pet adoptions. Shelter Hope Pet Shop has a unique, large-scale business model that aims to eliminate puppy mill pet shops in malls across the nation. Shelter Hope Pet Shop provides a fun, friendly place where visitors and volunteers can meet and interact with animals needing adoption. You can also visit Shelter Hope Pet Shop for pet merchandise and know your dollars are going directly back to help save the lives of homeless pets.

I parked the car and went in. Chip was a poodle mix and we hit it off right away, however I noticed that he had a buddy, Vince a cockapoo. The two just played together and immensely enjoyed each other's company. I could not bear to separate them, so both Vince and Chip were welcomed to my home. I had mistakenly left my cell phone at home and after introducing the boys to their new digs I heard my phone chirping to let me know there were unheard messages tucked away inside.

WHAT?!, I thought. Had I just heard the message correctly from Letty, that Lucky had been found? Pictures via text had been sent to Letty, which she forwarded to me. The pictures led me to believe—and to become very certain—the dog was really Lucky.

"Lucky's cry," Letty's voice excitedly said, "was a cry that only a mother knows." Letty was confident when the video arrived on her cell phone that this was the real deal.

Pictures were forwarded to Lucky's vet, Dr. Yale in Temecula and he too agreed that it would seem that this was Lucky, as his missing teeth and bottom lower jaw were distinct matches. In the homemade video from the phone, Lucky was on a red leash, nearly unrecognizable, as his hair had become long and dirty, and covered his eyes. And he was being handled like a rag doll or stuffed animal as they tugged at his muzzle and nose to get him to show his teeth and jaw for recognition. Then a boy picked him up roughly and stretched him out, dangling him by his two front feet so that the person filming could show that Lucky had been fixed. I could tell from the short video these people did not care the least about Lucky.

What is most incredible and ironic is that the very exact day that I had given up hope and adopted two new amigos, my prayers had been answered.

I was speechless and gave thanks to the Lord.

May 8th

Post 201: Jim - Lucky; I just received a response from the

San Carlos highway billboard. The news is good and the pictures, the videos, shots of his upper and lower teeth are all in line. Lucky's veterinarian has compared his teeth x-rays with a still of the video and has replied, "There is a high probability this is him."

I'm pretty excited about traveling back and very likely being reunited. I could be with him this time next week. Please lift this up in your prayers. Jim

Post 202: IronwoodChef - Jim I do not know you, but I must applaud you on your relentless efforts to find your best friend **Lucky.**

I know it hurts a lot and more as time goes by, and I know he is also hurting without you and he can't wait to be back with his best friend also. I hope this all turns out for the best!

When I lost "Ozzy" a few years ago the hurt has not stopped and still brings tears to my eyes often. Stay Strong and God Bless, Sal F.

Post 203: Caroline - Jim, when you are reunited with LUCKY, a huge cheer will go up from San Carlos. I talked with you during the early days of your search and have been praying since. I am the one who suggested you contact all the dog groomers as another step in finding your boy. It doesn't seem you missed any chance to find your little guy.

My three rescue dogs mean the world to me too, and I cannot even imagine losing one of them. My little Sophia looks a lot like Lucky, but I rescued her over seven years ago at the Arizona Animal Rescue League in Phoenix. Little Lucie had been abandoned and wandering for months after Jimena flooded many areas around San Carlos and Little Charlie was being hawked on the street around San Carlos. Each of them are as attached to me, as I am to them.

Hope you have a joyous reunion as soon as you can get here to identify your boy. Please send me a PM to let me know how it goes. Maybe our little fur people can get together to play and celebrate your reunion. Caroline

May 9th

Post 204: Cathy1 - Great idea Caroline! Wouldn't a doggie party to celebrate be fun? Please let all of us know if Lucky is found. It has been a journey of pain around the heart for Jim and for all of us who love our pets.

Post 205: Porsche - A dog parade with the mascot being Lucky.

Post 206: GeorgeInSanCarlos - A dog parade and a fund raiser for Lucky. Start at Baracuda Bob's and end on the beach at La Palapa. 200 dogs @ $10 per dog in a jar at La Palapa would cover the reward. I'll bring 3 dogs.

May 11th

Post 207: Fern – Jim, my heart is with you. My little "Tecate Lite" looks a lot like "Lucky" and I have been stopped a number of times while walking him to have people ask, "Is that Lucky?" I say, "No, Tecate is quite a bit larger, but sure looks like Lucky." My heart would break if Tecate were kidnapped. Yes, let's have a 'doggie get-together' when your Lucky returns. Smiles, Fern

May 14th

Post 208: Sheilasu - Hi Jim, I am still praying that you get reunited with your sweet baby. All the best, and George, I love your idea - when Lucky is reunited with his Dad, we should indeed have a dog parade with $10 entry fee to cover the cost of the reward and if there are extra funds, donate them to the dog groups here in San Carlos.

11. A Community's Lucky Day?

I was ecstatic, but at the same time terrified that once again, disappointment would abound. I couldn't sleep in peaceful rest before because of the turmoil and turbulence of semi-consciousness; I always looked for Lucky, even in my dreams, always getting near and then nothing, a dead end and back to the beginning. An everlasting nightmare was my greeting as I closed my eyes for much-needed rest. *Perhaps I am close, even though I am yet more than 1,000 miles from where Lucky is and even further from the safety of the San Carlos community that I must leave behind*, I'd think. I'd traveled 700 miles from my home in the U.S., to venture 300 more miles into the state of Sinaloa, the drug cartel capital of Mexico; Sinaloa, where some of the most ruthless drug lords in the world spend their days terrorizing neighborhoods, selling their evil, mind-altering drugs throughout Mexico, then return home to spend their evenings enjoying meals and family time with spouses and children.

I found out that if I wanted my dear Lucky, I would have to venture into Sinaloa and leave the "No Hassle Zone" of Sonora. The state of Sonora is known for its welcoming spirit and being tourist-friendly towards U.S. citizens and our Canadian neighbors to the north. Federales there are more understanding with foreigners than they are with their own full-time, permanent residents of Mexico.

I contacted the U.S. Embassy in Hermosillo when given no alternatives from Lucky's ransom holders other than to venture into Los Mochis, Sinaloa for the exchange. The questions had always been the same, "Do you have the money? You will have $2,000.00 U.S. dollars on you, no?"

May 16th – Day 77 which is 539 Dog Days

Post 209: Jim - Good morning!

Well! Stop drinking your coffee and put down your donuts!

I have Lucky!

He seems well and responsive. Tomorrow I will be taking him to the veterinarian for a checkup and if everything is thumbs up, he's off to the groomer.

My heartfelt thanks to everyone, for your thoughts, comments, support and prayers. This was a tough journey, but also an awesome experience. The bonds of friendship that were made during this time will never be forgotten.

My special thanks to:

Letty Armenta

Alvaro and Lupita Limon Leon

Jorge Armenta

Armando

Jorge Pompa

City of San Carlos

City of Guaymas

Veterinarians of Hermosillo

Rescue centers in San Carlos, Guaymas and Hermosillo

Jon and Jen Hildebrand

Mark and his wonderful daughter Olivia in Obregon

Good Night. God Bless, Jim Kawaguchi

Post 210: Porsche - Have been praying for this for so long. We are having a dog parade with Lucky at the helm. This warms my heart. YEAH!

Post 211: GeorgeInSanCarlos – Like ☺ ☺👍☺👍

Post 212: Marlinmaster - WHOOOOO HOOOOOO! Great news Jim!

Post 213: Kokua - Dog Parade! Do you know what happened to him? Where he's been all this time? Leslie S.

Post 214: Joe - What an incredible story about Lucky and his dedicated pet parent! I must admit, I was doubtful Jim would ever see Lucky again. Jim's unwavering efforts and the fine support he received from so many folks along this journey are things I won't soon forget. Jim, I don't know you personally, but hope to meet you (and Lucky) sometime in the future. This news is a wonderful way to start my day! Joe

Post 215: Dweller - I am so happy for you, your persistence in getting him back was so admirable, that reunion I am sure is unforgettable in every way. Looking forward to that dog parade and meeting you and your best friend.

Post 216: mathis47 - Makes my day. So very happy for you and Lucky. What a monumental effort by you and others. CONGRATULATIONS.

Post 217: Mary - Details please. What led to his recovery and who received the reward?

Post 218: Jim - Attached is a picture of Lucky. (attached picture of Lucky standing on tile floor ungroomed and looking confused)

Post 219: mach1 - Great news!! You're right, what a wonderful way to start the day! So happy for both of you, Donna C.

Post 220: PobreBurro - Awesome! Congratulations to you and all who participated in this effort.

Post 221: PT - Way to go, Lucky is back ☺☺ at home again ☺

Post 222: Jim - Dr. Orasco gave Lucky a "thumbs up"! Dehydrated, a bit underweight; but, given time he is going to be walking through Barracuda Bob's meeting everyone! Off to groomer tomorrow. Thanks! Jim (attached photo of Dr. Orasco checking out Lucky at his office)

Post 223: bobnliz – Well, this is wonderful. Now, for those of us who have been faithfully following this story, would someone puh-leeze tell us HOW Lucky came to be found? Thanks, Lizzy

Post 224: Jim - Tonight I will share the story. Glad to relax here in San Carlos.

Post 225: MarlinMonroe - Jim and Lucky, So happy for the two of you. You worked so hard and it is amazing you were able to recover your buddy. When our now 90# Diesel was a pup, some teens walking through the neighborhood actually tried to reach through our wrought iron fencing and pick him up over the top to steal him. Our neighbors saw them and they gave up when they knew they were seen. We were actually in our house with the gate locked and they tried to take him from the back of the house. They have no idea how much peril they were in if I had seen them, it would have been a "life changing event" for all three of them. Cuddle your boy for all of us that have followed your story. M.M.

May 17th
Post 226: FishingSanCarlos – OH Jim, what a wonderful way to start our day. THANK YOU and LUCKY for letting us know that you have been re-united. I prayed every day that you would find Lucky. I thought of the sadness that you both felt being so far apart. I kept thinking how depressing it was for Lucky having to live with these STRANGE PEOPLE. I was scared every time I thought of what every day was like for him.

Jim,   you   are   an   inspiration   for   all
of   us   --   you   did   everything   RIGHT.
Love, Jennifer and Jon

Post 227: Ja - I must say, some people don't even look for their lost child as Jim has for Lucky. Ja

Post 228: Sylvie - So happy I'm crying!
Sylvie L.

Post 229: rattletrap99 - I'm just now checking out this thread. I saw the many signs around about Lucky and once checked out a dog I thought might be him, but it turned out to have a collar and belonged to the lady she was with. Anyway, I'd also be interested in how he came to be found.

Post 230: Starfish - All of us with prayers in our hearts for Lucky's safe return are rejoicing with you tonight. We hope when you are rested and well, you will share your story of victory. It will be such a validation of all our prayers and positive thoughts. It is such a happy ending to such a frightening story, the happy ending provides a lift of hope to all our hearts? Good things can happen.

Post 231: SanCarlosMaverick - Jim, you should have heard Olivia's screams of joy when I told her that you and Lucky were back together. We are coming to San Carlos for a wedding reception at Bonafacios in two weeks, so we would love to stop by and see you and Lucky. You are to be admired for your dedication and persistence, which is the reason for this successful conclusion. I think those of us who offered our help fed off of that boundless hope, dedication, and persistence. It was an excellent learning experience for Olivia, me, and many others to "Never give up!" Our prayers were answered! See you soon,

Mark and Olivia (Team Lucky de Obregon)

Post 232: Jim - Here is Lucky, all nice and cleaned up. No mohawk for the "perritas," but it will grow back! We spent most of the day being lazy on the couch and sleeping. Late this afternoon he sat "shotgun" with me and we cruised San Carlos.

Last, I really wanted to say; "I'm sorry for not Posting his story yet." I'm just really lazy and still in a surreal moment. Also, I only have a cell phone to communicate with on this visit. It's going to be a few days to do this. I'll be Posting a few pictures and updating over the next few days.

Good night and God Bless all of you! I love San Carlos! James Kawaguchi

May 18th

Post 233: Jim - Lucky all spiffed up. (image attached of Lucky all cleaned up and his tail high in the Mexico sky)

Post 234: Marlinmaster - Lookin' good Lucky, get your Parade face on!!

Post 235: Jim - Lucky cruisin' the marina in Jon Hildebrand's quiet and smooth, electric boat. (image attached of Lucky riding proud in the boat, wind blowin through his hair)

Post 236: Starfish - Surely, you can share the miracle of recovering Lucky soon. So many of us have prayed, supported, and searched. It would be a sweet reward to find out how Lucky was recovered, as well as offer future strategies for the next one to lose their little 4-legged buddy. Wishing you and Lucky many, more, happy years together.

Post 237: DonJaime - With a dozen dogs of my own, I recognize the smile of contentment on Lucky's face with his family.

Post 238: DonJaime - Why do you Post

S
I
D
E
W
A
Y
S

Not Cool! (Author's note: this is referring to some of the pictures of Lucky that Jim had Posted which came up sideways on the thread.)

Post 239: Sheilasu - I am so happy to hear that you found your pal Lucky, and that he is back with you, where he belongs. You are to be commended for never giving up on your fur baby; he is lucky to have you. I haven't read all the messages, but noticed something about a parade, I know many folks who would love to meet sweet Lucky (and you), and to help, even in a small way, with the cost of the reward paid. All the best.

Post 240: Mary – Especially, if we ever hear the story of how he was rescued.

May 19th
Post 241: gbates - I think he explained the reason, only way to Post this trip is by cell phone.

Post 242: Ja - TO ME, This thread is a letdown NOW.
Jim you had 100s of people praying, helping and on their tip toes waiting for you to fine Lucky.
We all remember how Alfred Hitchcock movies ended. OUR GUESS. Dad hated A.H. 30 mins. time on Black/ White TV, back in the 50's.

You had time to keep this going for weeks on end. Please find time to tell us the end of your tour looking for Lucky. You'll make a lot of people happy to read the REAL end of the story. Ja, Larry

GOOD IDEA gbates, We need Jim's cell number so 100s of us can call him. Real Mexican way to do it. Wasted time and money on the phone.

Post 243: gbates - Give Jim a break. He will reply when he has a computer available and is emotionally ready to tell his story.

Post 244: gbates - I may have not been clear with my Post. He said he only had cell phone this trip to Post. No computer.

Post 245: MexicoMel – I am sure there are many people in San Carlos that would allow him to use their computer so the story could be told. He is more than welcome to use one of mine Nytime (sic) he sees fit. MexicoMel

Post 246: MexicoMel - Oops! "Anytime."

Post 247: gbates - When a person goes through a very emotional situation they need to take the time to process and heal before it is comfortable for them to write about their experience. Your need to know does not trump his need to deal with it in his own time. The dog is safe, and at home, that is the only thing that matters!

Post 248 – GeorgeInSanCarlos - The message below should be sufficient. If and when Jim wants to share his experience he will. Please folks, a little respect please. (Author's note: George has rePosted below what Jim had written earlier as a way of sending a message to the impatient ones that Jim had thanked them and that should be good enough.)

Good morning!

Well! Stop drinking your coffee and put down your donuts!

I have Lucky!

He seems well and responsive. Tomorrow I will be taking him to the veterinarian for a checkup and if everything is thumbs up, he's off to the groomer. My heartfelt thanks to everyone for your thoughts, comments, support and prayers. This was a tough journey but also an awesome experience. The bonds of friendship that were made during this time will never be forgotten.

My special thanks to:
Letty Armenta
Alvaro and Lupita Limon Leon
Jorge Armenta
Armando
Jorge Pompa
City of San Carlos
City of Guaymas
Veterinarians of Hermosillo
Rescue centers in San Carlos, Guaymas and Hermosillo
Jon and Jen Hildebrand
Mark and his wonderful daughter Olivia in Obregon
Good Night.
God Bless
Jim Kawaguchi

Post 249: FishingSanCarlos – Gretchen, thank you so much for having the HEART that you have. Jim is a good friend to Jon and I, and we talked to Jim, but don't know the details. It is very hard for him right now, the $2,000.00 is LAST on his mind. He is savoring the reality that he has LUCKY in his arms and it is very difficult to RELIVE the situation at this time. He will Post about the rescue of LUCKY when he is ready. He is right now re-acquainting with Lucky. Don't forget that Lucky went through so much agony. His time is spent right now re-assuring Lucky that this will NEVER happen again.

Give him some time to bond with his best friend and re-assure Lucky and himself that what they went through was a nightmare and had devastating effects on both of them. He does plan to give a detailed update, but let him ALONE for now with LUCKY.

Thanks, Jon and Jennifer

May 26th

Post 250: davev1 - OK Now we are on page 10, how about how Lucky was found and the WHOLE story? Is it a big secret? How? When?

May 27th

Post 251: Tropicalgirl - Congratulations Jim and Lucky. I'm so happy that Lucky is home where he belongs. Big hugs to you both from Canada. Yup, the good news is spreading to those of us who have gone home for the summer.

May 29th

Post 252: Rico1 - Yes, Jim got "Lucky" by being persistent and never giving up on finding his "little buddy." Thank GOD, Goodness & the people of Mexico, especially San Carlos, Guaymas, Empalme, Hermosillo & Obregon!

Rico Austin

Post 253: Jim - Hi Everyone!

Lucky now has a web page (it's very simple and in the works so just check it out!) and soon there will be much more to read. Also, Lucky will have a Facebook page so you can be free to browse and comment on his latest Postings.

For your surprise please go to: http://www.MexicoGot-Lucky.com and print your copy, sign your sheet and give to the host.

Lucky's gift will be available on Sunday, June 1st and will

continue through July 30th.

1 per person.

Thanks Again! Jim

May 30th

Post 254: Jim - Hi Folks!

Lucky says, "Pick up your free cup of coffee at Barracuda Bob's starting on Sunday!"

Saludos, Jim Kawaguchi

Post 255: gbates - How very nice!

May 31st

Post 256: Jim - Good Morning!

Lucky says, "Remember to pick up your free small coffee at Barracuda Bob's tomorrow!"

http://www.mexicogotlucky.com

(*Author's note*: Jim had placed a coupon on Lucky's new website which each person in San Carlos could print off and turn in for a free cup of coffee.)

August 1st

Post 257: Rico1 - To All: The Book "Mexico got Lucky" is nearly done and ready to go to the publisher! Thank You for all Your help & support and for Jim never giving up on finding his Boy, Mr. Lucky!

Post 218.
Lucky is
finally home.

Post 222. Dr. Orasco giving Lucky a much needed check-up.

Post 233. Lucky all spiffed up & extremely happy.

Post 235. Lucky crusin' the marina in Amigo John's boat.

12 🐾 The Exchange, $26,000 Pesoes to get Lucky!

The first text I received showed Lucky, the next text posed the ominous question: "Do you have the money? $2,000 in cash?"

I nervously responded back, "Yes, I have the money, we will be there at 5:00." I wondered if we were doing the right thing or were we driving right into a dark trap that has seen its share of hombres disappearing into the black hole of Mexico, never to be heard from or seen again. I shuddered at this thought and many others just as disturbing, nearly the same time as did my phone, "We have LUCKY!" Was that a threat or a warning, or an assurance? Not only was there a cultural and language barrier, but, one of the dark side of thieves versus the good side of normal, average, everyday abiding citizens. There was no way of knowing what was actually meant by their last text; but, I would have to take it as all three combined and of each on its own separate merit. I did hope and pray that they would believe that no funny business, no heroics, no double cross was on my mind or in our plans.

Big Al (Alvardo) had outlined a plan that we meet the ransom holders along *Ruta* 15 (Highway 15) where there is a *cuota* (toll booth) as there would be armed guards nearby, in case things turned beyond our control. We talked it over and decided against it for three reasons: (1) Most likely the dognappers would hesitate in rendezvousing in such a military and government setting. (2) If something did run amiss—usually bad people have weapons with them and the military personnel have weapons—one wrong move by the negotiating thieves could send bullets into the air and into our bodies. (3) If Lucky's controllers did not like the look of the layout, they could easily turn, run, hide, and perhaps that would be the end for Lucky and for our reunion.

No, it was out of the ruling, we needed to suggest and agree to a more neutral meeting place for "the exchange."

There was an OXXO convenience store on the north side of Los Mochis where we would meet at 5:00 p.m. with promises of no questions, no police, no tricks. It was a six-hour drive for us from San Carlos to Los Mochis. We wanted to get there a couple hours early to case the place, scope out all the exits, side streets, just to be on the safe and prepared side of what unknowns were in our near future as our car and lives left the safety of San Carlos and Sonora at 9:00 a.m. and ventured across the state line into the drug cartel-controlled state of Sinaloa.

Lupita and Letty were side by side with Big Al and me as we headed south, through Guaymas, Empalme, and then entered into neighboring Sinaloa. The moment we entered into Sinaloa our moods changed from trusting to being wary. All four of us knew that we had entered into a realm of Mexico like no other.

The Sinaloa Cartel is the most powerful drug trafficking, money laundering and organized crime syndicate on the globe. This cartel is based in the city of Culiacán, Sinaloa which is just a mere two hours south of where we were meeting the dog thieves. Who knew what or who else they might be involved in or with. The U.S. Intelligence Community speaks of the Sinaloa Cartel as "the most powerful drug trafficking organization in the world." *The Los Angeles Times* called the Cartel, "Mexico's most powerful organized crime group," and we were headed straight into the open arms of Mexican opium and marijuana fields.

Just days before Lucky was stolen, "El Chapo" Guzman was arrested in February of 2014 at a beachfront condo in Mazatlán, an hour south of Guzman's full-time residence in Culiacán, Sinaloa. Señor Guzman had been on the lam since escaping federal prison in 2001, still the mighty leader of the Sinaloa Cartel. There was little doubt in my mind, they (his gang) would find a way for him to find freedom again. It could only be a matter of time, before "El Chapo" would escape the Mexican prison system once more, to live in hiding, lurking and leading the drug cartel, somewhere within the state of Sinaloa. Now perhaps you understand a little clearer, the dangerous circumstances and can appreciate the anxiety the four of us felt, just a bit more.

I was scared, on the edge of terrified. I was extremely uneasy and frightened about involving three other innocent, good, God-fearing people into "the exchange."

The drive went without fanfare and every once in a while, Big Al would look over and give me a thumbs up indication and say, "Don't worry Jim, we'll get Lucky back," all with a big grin on his lovable-looking face.

We found the OXXO convenience store, which is the equivalent of Circle K or 7-11 convenience stores in the United States. We arrived just after 3:00 p.m., so had plenty of time to get a good layout of the land before our meeting. We strategically placed our car for easy access and a quick get-away if the circumstances led to that choice.

At five minutes until 5:00 p.m., three different women showed up, two coming from one direction and the other from another. It was show time. As Big Al and I made our way carefully across to the sidewalk, we saw a police car off to the right which was a godsend for us. Two of the gals had Lucky on a leash while the third gal was about twenty yards away talking into her cell phone, both of her watchful eyes intently on the two of us.

Letty and Lupita were in the car with an excellent vantage point, doors were locked and windows were rolled entirely up in the car. Letty was in perfect position to be able to take photographs and video. Lupita had her cell next to her beating chest, ready to call the policía in an instant, if things went south.

Al and I approached the one lady, who looked to be in her early thirties. She looked to be much older of the two. This gal pulled back on Lucky's leash and started arguing with the younger girl who looked to be about eighteen years of age. We could tell immediately the two women did not trust each other, let alone the two strangers who wanted nothing more than to get their dog and get the heck out of Los Mochis, Sinaloa.

We backed off and glanced over at the third woman who was now directly behind us, about twenty-five feet, still appearing to be talking on her cell phone, though she never took those dark, menacing eyes off us, for even a moment of time.

Big Alvardo spoke in Spanish and asked how they were doing, he told them that we had the money. I had a white envelope stuffed with twenty of the Franklin hundreds of U.S. currency. I approached Lucky, he did not respond to my voice or to my touch, but, as I inspected him, I knew it to be him. He was still sporting the red Disney tag that I had given him for our last

Christmas together. Lucky could not see me from under the matted, dirty hair covering his eyes and he did not recognize my voice. I was confused as to what was going on. My Lucky could not have forgotten about me this quickly or could he have? Or perhaps, was he so traumatized, that his memory had been selectively damaged?

I asked how long they had had Lucky and the response was two months. They claimed to have had purchased my boy for $100 dollars U.S. This sounded like the lie that it was. Why would anyone in Mexico pay $100 for a dog that could not breed and was not full bred? If a person was really to spend that kind of money for a dog, wouldn't they take care of him, water him, feed him, bathe him, and at the very least trim his hair from his eyes so that he could see? Yes, they were dog thieves, we both knew it and they knew we knew that their story was bogus. Never in my life have I ever wanted to punch three human beings so much. I could barely stand to look at their vile faces as I could see touches of evil reeking stench from all three of the female souls and bodies.

The women (although this term should not be used to describe the three inhumane humans) were probably going nuts in their heads, thinking, *this is not the dog that we thought he was, he doesn't recognize his owner, we have been set up.* All three of the females were now as nervous as Al and me. I was afraid things were about to turn bad, however, there was one thing I hadn't done yet and that was sing to Lucky. We had a private little song that was just between the two of us. I would sing "I love you" a couple of times and then Lucky would try to sing back. "I love you" would come out as part cry, part howl and then I would sing to Lucky again. We'd go back and forth. To the astonishment of the women and Al, I started to sing, "I love you" and instantly Lucky's ears perked up, his tail went straight for the air and he sang back, "I love you."

A miracle indeed! I grabbed Lucky, handed the older woman the envelope and we made quick, double time steps for the car. Al backed away so that he could keep an alert eye on all of the thieves. Lupita had already turned the ignition over in the car and had hit the unlock button. Al and I both swung open the car doors and each of us, with one quick motion were in the car. Al was safe in the driver's seat and I right behind him in the backseat with Lucky in my arms. As we sped out of the lot, I looked back over my shoulder and the three vile humans were huddled together, counting their evil, ransom money that no goodness or honesty could ever purchase.

We raced out of town with Letty and I every now and then, looking back over our shoulders. I watched a calm Al behind the steering wheel check his rear-view mirror many times to make sure that we were not followed from Los Mochis. There were no cars on our tail.

After we got out of town, I was ecstatic to have my old friend back in my arms, where he belonged. Alvardo put his hand back behind the seat for me to touch in celebration and said, "We got your little buddy back," and then the large man chuckled which set the other three of us into joyous laughter and tears of "can you believe it?!"

We did not stop until we reached Obregón, about three and a half hours north of Los Mochis. Lucky had been very quiet during the ride and seemed to be still confused as to what this car ride meant, still not fully understanding that he was safe with me. After making sure we were not followed, we stopped at an open-air eatery for tacos. Lucky loves tacos and he gulped his dinner and the water up more quickly than I had ever witnessed him eating food or lapping up water before.

Arriving into the safe haven of San Carlos around midnight, I carried Lucky into the house and set him down on the tile floor. He immediately started sniffing around excitedly, recognizing old scents and refamiliarizing himself with his humble abode. After nearly an hour of this, he went to his bed, and laid down. I cuddled up next to him. In a few, short minutes Lucky was sleeping soundly with no cares or nightmares and then I too fell, into a perfect, relaxed night of rest.

May 16th – Day 77 which is 539 Dog Days

The next morning I jumped out of bed, gave Lucky a hug, went into my study, opened my laptop, went to "My Favorites," found VivaSanCarlos. mx and gleefully typed the message below while giving thanks to the Lord, to Mexico, to San Carlos, to one of the greatest communities I've ever had the pleasure of being a part of, and of course, to all members of Team Lucky!

Post 209: Jim - Good morning!

Well! Stop drinking your coffee and put down your donuts!

I have LUCKY!

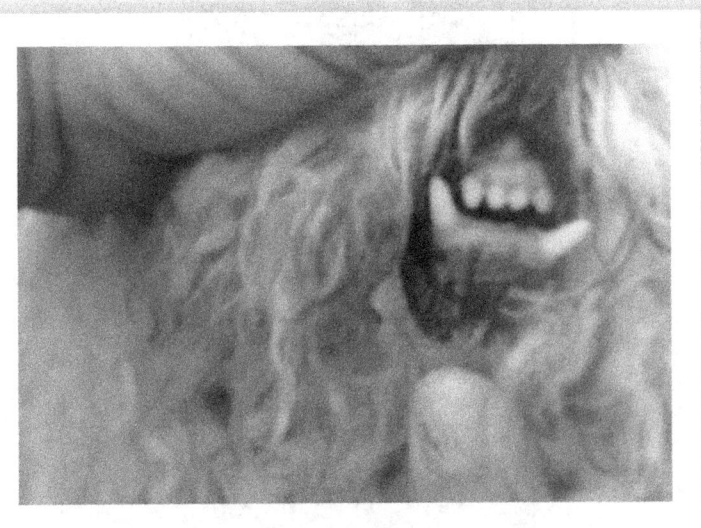

The Thief showing Lucky's teeth.

The Exchange: Jim & Lucky singing (I love you).

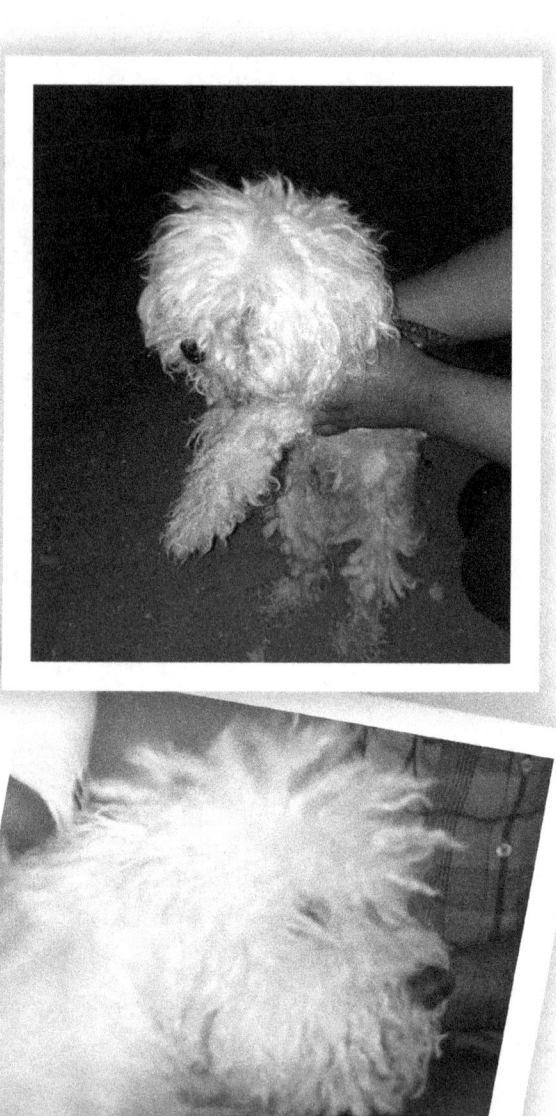

Doing the hand off in Los Mochis.

Lucky safe on Jim's lap.

 *Epilogue*

May 16ᵗʰ, 2014

Latitude: 27.58 degrees North
Longitude 111.06 degrees West

As I lounge lazily in a white plastic chair with a Mexican beer logo scrawled in red across the back, I watch a pair of jet skis whip zigzags about 200 feet from the shore in the Sea of Cortez. A group of seven tourists loudly enter the drinking establishment, one of them bold from the tequila from a previous watering hole is eager to use his newly learned Spanish vocabulary mixed with a word of English. He blurts obnoxiously, yet with a phrase of politeness to the waiter, "*Por favor, cinco cervezas and dos margaritas.*" I grin gently to myself, nod to the vacationers and quietly thank the Lord for this glorious, sun-filled day.

I'm chillaxin' at the beachside Soggy Peso AKA the Hangout, situated on the fairest stretch of white beach in the Mexican state of Sonora.

A couple miles northwest of San Carlos lies the soft, white, powdery sand of Algodones Playa (Cotton Beach) which is home to Playa Blanca Condos that rise 15 stories into the blue sky, also the five storied San Carlos Plaza Hotel Resort and less than half a dozen beach bars. The former Club Med, now known as Paradiso Resort Beach Club on one end and Playa Blanca at the other, act as borders to the Soggy Peso, La Salsa, Bonifacio's Cotton Club and possibly another one or two of which their names escape me. Bonafacio's main building has been refurbished, redecorated and renovated from its former self as the Night Club owned by and on the property of Club Mediterranean, a French owned corporation with vacation resorts found in many parts of the world, usually in exotic locations. These libation huts and palapas are so closely built to each other it is sometimes difficult to know where one property ends and another begins.

The reason I sit and waste away another beautiful day in paradise at Soggy Peso is because of loyalty; it was the first place established with musica and a refreshing cold drink this far from the small, but, growing tourist town of San Carlos. One half of my wooden table stands drenching in the sun, the other half is being cooled by the shade of the heavily thatched, woven, Mexican palm fronds. La Salsa and Bonifacio's Cotton Club are both great beachside watering holes with service that keeps a gal and guy returning. At those places and here is where you'll find the surfer looking dudes and dudettes that stole away from Arizona State or the University of Arizona for a three-day holiday break, fishermen of all sorts – weekend deep sea anglers, Alaskan crabbers enjoying the off season, and those that depend on a good day's catch nearly every day to pay the rent and afford the occasional cerveza alongside the tourists.

As I scan the crowd, I'm sure there might be a felon or two; an overworked doctor; an overpaid attorney; a stressed out educator; a lounging construction worker; a writer enjoying a tasty margarita laced with his favorite tequila and time spent away from the computer, while banging away another story in his head; a waitress who has been waiting for this deserving day in over six months, finally able to be on the receiving side of service with a smile; and perhaps another entrepreneur like myself, just wanting to see and listen to the sea wash gently wave upon wave to the shore.

The party of seven seem oblivious to others and their surroundings. To their credit, each of them were enjoying life and the simple pleasures thereof.

My attention is drawn to the West as the sun has begun to settle on the ocean, dancing with sparkles of light jolting from the slight ripples of the calm sea. In just a matter of seconds I take a snapshot with my phone before it is lost, only to be found in the eastern skies in the form of a sunrise.

The young-looking, grayish, white-haired musician wearing shorts, a short-sleeve shirt with Hawaiian print, standing in sandals, picks up his guitar in front of the primitive stage made up of a slab of concrete and bamboo poles tied together with strands of strong, weedy grass standing vertically as a backdrop. "Hey, how about that sunset behind me! I'm Mexico Mark and ... ."

I look at my curly, white buddy enjoying his late afternoon nap, lounging in the shadow of the table with the soft sand beneath his body. I glance over at the mural painted on the wall that reads, "Latitude 27.58 Degrees North, Longitude 111.06 Degrees West," and I smile.

Buenas noches,
Jim

Eric Holland
www.facebook.com/erichollandaz

Mark Mulligan
www.markmulligan.net/

Sam Rainwater & Mark Mulligan
playing Charity Concert for Castaway Kids.

Bobby & Leslie Sahlen
www.stockmusicsite.com/BobbyLeslieSahlen

Sam Rainwater
www.samlrainwater.com/music.htm

Eric Holland

Ronald Vogelsang Daisley
www.facebook.com/RonaldVogelsangDaisley

Eric Holland
www.facebook.com/erichollandaz

Lorena Robles.
www.facebook.com/pages/Lorena-Robles-Cantante/315868248512048

Mexico Mark, Tequila Rico & San Carlos Lenny
in Laughlin NV at Phins to the West!

Author Rico Austin at Soggy Peso Bar.

Jim Kawaguchi & Rico Austin celebrating
Lucky's return to San Carlos.

July 4th, 2014

A few of Lucky's fans, supporters & those that searched nonstop
for the most famous dog in Sonora, Mexico are celebrating
his safe return of an incredible and dangerous journey.

Photo courtesy of Overland Photography

2

🐾 A New Beginning for 🐾 Dogs

1 🐾"Rescue a dog, you won't regret it" — Rico Austin

I found this Post below on VivaSanCarlos.mx on September 30, 2013. I believe it says volumes about the dirty world of puppy mills that exist in order to get pure bred dogs for mankind who are willing to pay.

Please, I urge each and every one of you to consider going to a dog pound, to a shelter and adopting or rescuing a dog or puppy. Please do not purchase one at the mall or a pet store as this behavior fans the flames of those breeding dogs and cats for profit.

Meet the Mother of Your Pet Store Puppy
From Vicky's Pet-setting

"My name is 109. I have lived in a puppy mill for six years. I have had 11 litters of puppies and made my owner over $30,000.00. To show his gratitude, he has never bathed or brushed me, he has never placed a kind hand on me. I have never seen a vet or felt grass under my feet. The only time I am out of my 2x3 crate is when I am bred by force. I get a little more food and a cleaner pen when I have my babies. I am happy for a while; but, by four weeks they take my pups away to sell them online, at pet stores and I am alone again, back in my crate. The wire floor in my pen has caused me to have permanent deep painful groves in my pads. My nails are so long I can't walk on a hard surface. Today, we were rescued! I am so scared, but I experienced something I have never heard before, a soft gentle voice."[1]

---

1 https://m.facebook.com/Vickys-Pet-sitting-433002650226042/

2 The "Mother Teresa of Dogs"

I met Barb in August 2014 as part of research for this book. I had heard of a woman who had lived in Scottsdale, and was a successful realtor who had sold her home, her land and eventually most everything she owned, to move to Rocky Point to help find homes and care for stray and unwanted dogs.

The drive from Scottsdale, AZ to Rocky Point AKA Puerto Peñasco, Sonora, Mexico is not the most pleasant of road trips in mid-August, especially when no monsoons are in the near forecast. For those of you who have never been to Rocky Point, it is the closest point by car to reach the Sea of Cortez from the Phoenix/Scottsdale area.

I drove into Rocky Point only to learn that I had passed Barb's Dog Rescue by eight miles, located just off Highway 8, which is the main highway where the Lukeville/Sonoyta border crossing is located and continues on into the dusty, resort town of Rocky Point. There is a sign of which I missed, that is somewhere between Kilometers 85-87 that guides you on a long driveway to the trailer and kennels where Barb and her 101 dogs breathe and eat. Actually, I believe there were sixty-nine dogs on hand the day that I met the woman whom some called the "Mother Teresa of Dogs."

Dogs barking, tails wagging and the hot sun baking, I pulled up to the enclosed fencing of where I literally saw nearly a hundred dogs, all clamoring for attention. There were even a couple of strays that came running over from on an adjacent property to greet me, craving for a pat on the head, a kind word.

Barb stepped out of the trailer holding a small puppy and waved hello to me. After introductions were made, I explained to Barb why I had come and told her most of the story of "Lucky" the stolen dog in Sonora, and of the book I was writing. The spry 70 plus-year-old woman then shared most of her life story with me and said with a smile, "So strange that you came by today. See this little guy here that I'm holding? He was brought to me today by a worker that helps me here at the rescue part-time. This morning while he was getting ready to leave his home in Rocky Point he heard a whimpering coming from the garbage dumpster next to his home, and this poor little pup was in there. Can you believe someone just threw this poor, innocent, little creature into the waste, knowing that he would probably die?"

But before I could answer, she continued on, "I named him 'Lucky' because he is darn lucky to be alive, and now here you are, doing a story on a dog named 'Lucky.'" Yes, what a coincidental world we reside in.

I took many pictures, scratched many a dog behind the ear, and patted their backs before saying adios to Barb. She thanked me for coming to see her, for writing the book, *Mexico got Lucky*, and for bringing more needed attention to dog rescues and spaying. Barb did not ask me for a donation, and as I was getting in the car to leave, it dawned on me that I had not offered any financial help. I dug into my Levi's, pulled some bills from my money clip, and gave her a small cash donation of which I have no doubt in my mind she stretched as far as she could for the animals for which she cared. I could tell by the way she dressed, the way she lived, the way she talked: her first priority was in helping each and every dog find a home.

Now, a bit more about this saint of a lady.

Barb was a very successful real estate broker serving the Scottsdale market. Many years ago, Barb had lost her twenty-one-year-old daughter in an auto accident, and we can only try and imagine her pain. She visited Rocky Point, Mexico for a long weekend getaway for rest about fifteen years ago and saw the desperate need for animal assistance there. Barb was overcome with sadness at what she saw: skinny, dying dogs begging for any scrap, for an ounce of water. She knew at that telling moment her calling on Earth was to help animals find good, nurturing homes.

A year later after having liquidated her assets, she returned to Rocky Point and began what would become her lifetime quest of helping unwanted dogs. Barb didn't purchase some luxurious mansion or resort home along the Sea of Cortez; no, she opted for an inexpensive piece of land with no shade, no sight of the ocean, only white sand and dirt for miles. Barb's Dog Rescue (a non-profit) headquarters was on a piece of land with a small mobile home (AKA trailer house) and kennels that she had built on the property. For nine and a half years she supported the rescue with no outside help, which included offering food, housing, veterinary care, spay and neutering, and FREE adoption services. That's right FREE! Barb continued this until she ran out of her own money and had nothing left to sell. Only at this time did she begin to ask for donations and help.

Barb and her dog rescue rely totally on American donations for their continued existence. She has an urgent need for food and medical supplies as the shelter is just about out of food and medicines at the time of this writing. You will see her yellow signs north of Rocky Point (miles north of the round intersection that goes to Caborca). Look for her signs and take her a few big bags of dog food and puppy food, or donate on her website. She cares for 70+ dogs and puppies. She hopes to expand her facility. She is 70+ years old—incredible! The "Mother Teresa of Dogs." She also has her website on her signs to donate to as well; you can see it in this YouTube video about her rescue: https://www.youtube.com/watch?v=0oKLKXD-jKPY .

Please help her any way you can, so she can continue her mission of serving man's best friend!

Sources:
http://www.barbsdogrescuerp.com/
https://www.facebook.com/BarbsDogRescue?fref=ts
https://www.youtube.com/watch?v=0oKLKXDjKPY

Concerned about a stray dog?
Please contact Barb! She and the Rescue will do their best to help.
Email: BarbsDogRescue@gmail.com
Barb's Mexico Cell: 638-114-1659
International Call from the US: 011-52-1-638-114-1659
US Phone Number: 602-774-1578

Barb's Dog Rescue, Puerto Penasco, Sonora, Mexico

Barb with new puppy Lucky!
"Mother Teresa of Dogs"

Barb's home & Dog Rescue.

Some of Barb's Dogs wanting attention & homes.

Dogs coming to greet Rico.

See the Dog standing, he wants to play ball.

Rico saw this Perro Bandito vehicle on the beach in Rocky Point.

Lucky the most famous dog in Sonora, even has a cantina.

3 Caboholics & Cabo Helping Pets

I belong to a social group on Facebook called the Caboholics Support Group, of which I have been a member for a few years now. I believe I joined Facebook in the summer of 2009 and joined the group shortly after that. I became a bonafided Caboholic. This group was created by Johnny and Maddie Haney (AKA Johnny and Maddie Corona) to help all Caboholics cope with the day-to-day struggles of Caboholism. Each time a person vacations in Cabo the group grows. The desire for your next "fix" is much stronger than it was after your last trip. You may find yourself flying down for a "quick last-minute trip" more often than you ever thought you would.

There are two Caboholic Conventions per year where we party, we socialize, we boat, we dance, we fish, we donate money and we volunteer time to a few non-profit organizations that either help homeless animals or children without families and normal home lives, some of us even hang out and help raise money for *bomberos* (firefighters). Members are welcome and encouraged to ask questions, share news, special events, links, photos, videos, stories about their favorite restaurant, bar, places, etc.

You can join the group here: https://www.facebook.com/groups/caboholics/?fref=ts

Below are websites and descriptions of dog shelters in Cabo.

El Ranchito in San Jose is a dog rescue run by two girls, Nereyda and Mariana. Visit https://www.facebook.com/elranchitocabo/?ref=page_internal

Voluntarios de Corazon. You can learn more through visiting their Facebook page at https://www.facebook.com/pages/Voluntarios-de-Cora-z%C3%B3n/193549044002017

The Los Cabos Humane Society & Adoption Center is dedicated to providing the community with animal control services and to creating an environment free of homeless dogs and cats. Los Cabos Humane Society promotes the following: spaying and neutering, education, and adoption- Los Cabos Humane Society – Nonprofit organization: http://www.los-caboshumanesociety.com/index.html

The Los Cabos Humane Society & Adoption Center Quick Facts

From The Los Cabos Humane Society website[1]

Did you know the LCHS receives no government funding and that there is no animal control facility in the Los Cabos county? The LCHS is made up of a group of volunteers that work together to help promote and provide humane animal services for all of Los Cabos.

Did you know we have performed over 15,000 spay/neuter surgeries since 2011?

Did you know that we have taught our Education Program to thousands of children and adults regarding the Humane Treatment of Animals?

Did you know that we have provided happy homes to thousands of dogs and cats through our Adoption Program?

Our goal at the LCHS is to promote the humane treatment of domestic animals through education, pet population control, and adoption.

Thank you for being our "friend" and helping us to continue providing our services to the Los Cabos community.

Did you know the LCHS receives no government funding and that there is no animal control facility in the Los Cabos county? The LCHS is made up of a group of volunteers that work together to help promote and provide humane animal services for all of Los Cabos.

Did you know the LCHS receives no government funding and that there is no animal control facility in the Los Cabos county? The LCHS is made up of a group of volunteers that work together and help promote and provide humane animal services for all of Los Cabos.

Did you know that we have perfomed over 15,000 spay/neuter surgeries since 2011?

Did you know that we have taught our Education Program to thousands of children and adults regarding the Humane Treatment of Animals?

1 https://loscaboshumanesociety.org/

Did you know that we have provided happy homes for thousands of dogs and cats through our Adoption Program?

Our goal at the LCHS is to promote the humane treatment of domestic animals through education, pet population control and adoption.

Thank you for being "our friend" and helping us to continue providing our services to the Los Cabos community.

Due to the overwhelming number of owner-surrendered pets we are receiving every month, the Los Cabos Humane Society is forced to start asking for a fee to take them into the adoption center.

Starting August 1st we will ask for $100 pesos per pet that is surrendered. This amount only pays for 3-4 days of care at the adoption center. It does not cover testing, spay/neuter, adoption or continued care if the animal is not adopted quickly.

A pet is a responsibility for the entire life of that animal and should not be taken lightly. Please spay/neuter your pets and help us stop animal neglect and abuse.

Source:

https://www.facebook.com/pages/Los-Cabos-Humane-Society/333677670077275

HUMANE SOCIETY

LOS CABOS
Humane Society

Volunteers are welcome daily to
help walk the dogs or play with the
cats. Fun for the whole family!

EL RANCHITO

El Ranchito serves as a halfway home
home for dogs that need a little more
love & care before they are adoptable.

Gracias to all Caboholics
for your generous donations & volunteerism.

Caboholics Convention, February 2015

Rico with his Caboholic Amigas & Amigos!

Who Helped the Dogs Out? Who?   Who?

WE Did!!!

4   San Carlos & SBPA Cares

From The SBPA Organization in San Carlos website[1]

The Sociedad Benefactora y Proteccion Animal or SBPA Organization in San Carlos, Sonora, Mexico is dedicated to minimizing unwanted dog and cat populations by providing free Spay and Neuter Certificates to local, low-income families. It is also dedicated to the protection of animals, domestic and feral, and to the alleviation of suffering created by uncontrolled reproduction. We believe that spay and neuter is the best solution to the overpopulation problem.

We do not operate an animal shelter nor do we operate a veterinary care facility.

SBPA Services, Inc. is an Arizona non-profit 501(c)(3) corporation headquartered in Tucson, Arizona. The corporation's purpose is to provide services for the Sociedad Benefactora y Protección Animal (SBPA) A.C. in San Carlos, Nuevo Guaymas, Sonora, Mexico, its endeavors and related programs.

The goals of SBPA Services are to help with needed funding to cover expenses for spay and neuter clinics that are provided free of cost in the San Carlos area, to provide funding for vaccinations to reduce disease in the animal population. They also provide equipment, medical supplies, medicine, food and related items necessary for the continued operation of the Sociedad Benefactora y Proteccion Animal (SBPA) San Carlos A.C., a not for profit Mexican Civil Association, in its endeavors and related programs.

http://sbpasancarlos.org/

So far the SBPA has donated free surgical sterilizations for 700+ local

---

1 http://www.sbpasancarlos.com

dogs and cats.

"Altered Tails Book Shoppe" and SBPA Headquarters opened in 2013 and **YES! It's air conditioned.**

Three exciting new websites were created to showcase the many facets of our not-for-profit organization. Take a look at http://www.sbpasancarlos.com and link to the others to read our story.

Guess What the SBPA is Doing Now

Free Spay/Neuter Clinic for local dogs and cats scheduled:

Every penny and peso you donate at **"Altered Tails"** goes directly back to fund free spay and neuter clinics and to our local vets to prevent unwanted litters of cats & dogs.

To donate go to **PayPal** on our website or visit our **Facebook** page.

US dollar donations are tax deductible.

We're busy putting final touches on our **SBPA Calendar.**

Please support the SBPA - your local spay/neuter organization

Source:

https://www.facebook.com/pages/SBPA-San-Carlos/197277600418611

SBPA Book Shoppe next to Ruby Bar at the Marina in
San Carlos. Rico has donated his books here.

San Carlos Rescue Dogs, Paco & Pilar enjoying the
Sea of Cortez.

Join **SBPA** and Ruby Wine Bar

for the Happy Howloween Pooch Parade

Costumes, Dogs, and Sushi Oh My!!!

Thursday, October 30th

5PM Pooch Parade

6PM Sushi and Drink Specials

Prizes for Best Doggie Gear

Altered Tails Book Shoppe and Ruby Wine Bar - Marina San Carlos

Eat, drink and be SCARY

A portion of the proceeds will benefit the SBPA – your local spay & neuter non-profit

A fun event to raise money for dogs by SBPA & Ruby Bar which is named after Ruby the dog.

Ruby Bar owner Lisa, her Fisher Man Bryan with Paco & Pilar make up Team Margarita.

Lisa & Bryan saying "I Do" with man's best friend
(best man) Shaka, on the beach in San Carlos.

5 ❧ Education is the Answer

May 22, 2001

Jim: Good morning! I'll be calling around 9, if it's still good for you.

Rico: Si Señor! ;-)

That morning Jim had texted me at about 8:00 a.m. to make sure we were still on for our phone meeting.

At a few minutes past 9:00 a.m., I picked up the phone on its second ring and answered, "Good Morning, this is Rico."

"Hello Rico, Jim Kawaguchi here. How are you?"

"Super, and Amigo how are you doing? I'm very excited that you called and am looking forward to writing Lucky's story."

"Rico, first of all I want to thank you and your wife Connie for all the support, including your Facebook Posts and messages. I appreciate it very much; your willingness to write this short story for me so as to bring closure for the people of San Carlos and Guaymas that helped me get my Lucky back home to me."

"Jim, I am so happy and thankful that you are reunited with your boy Lucky, and I admire your persistence of never giving up the search. And thank you for the opportunity to share this story. Every writer dreams of getting a true story of this magnitude to write."

"I am so glad that you want to write this story. You were the first and only person that came to my mind of developing the short story. For me it was a natural, you're a great writer, you're well known in the San Carlos community. And you have followed Lucky's story from the beginning, sending me private messages of encouragement and disdain you held for the dog thieves."

The conversation continued and when Jim was telling me about the "kill centers" and describing the horrific conditions of the animals, my end of the phone was completely silent, as if no one were there on the line. What I had heard nearly took the breath and life from me; I was close to fainting as the pictures methodically ran through my mind, creating a canvas of blood mixed with starvation and uncleansed pens.

"Rico! Hello, Rico are you still there?"

"Yes Jim, I'm still here." Stuttering from the shock of what I had just heard, I continued, "I...I had no idea that the treatment of dogs in these so-called shelters was so harsh, and the brutality of hooking the dog up to a battery as a way of ending their poor, miserable lives. I'm just sick and I can only try to imagine the horrible images of what you saw in person, now with those pictures forever etched in your mind."

"Uh Rico, it was very sobering and to know that almost every single animal that I saw had a death sentence if not rescued or claimed by someone within a very few days. Those people at those facilities could care less about animals. Plus, they aren't given the resources of food, and they don't bother to water the dogs either. Yes, you are right, it is sickening to the sight."

"Jim, this is more than a short story, this is a book of two stories or parts: one of Lucky being stolen, of the persistent efforts of his dad and the people of San Carlos, Guaymas and of Mexico searching and bringing him home. The other is of education and of sharing the conditions and how these animals are put to an inhumane death. We can help to begin the education process for the Mexican people and especially to their and our younger generation of children. We can share the knowledge of the importance of spaying and neutering dogs and cats to prevent the many unwanted animals roaming the streets of most every small town and large city in Mexico. This is an opportunity to write a great dog-human interest story, and at the same time we can be doing something very worthwhile: The beginning of perhaps changing the way Mexico deals with unwanted or stray canines and felines."

"Wow! But, is this something you want to take on, writing a full book instead of just putting together a short story?"

"Absolutely! Jim, do you remember when we were kids, how much trash there was along the highways and littering was rampant among most people? It was nothing to see someone throw their pop bottle or McDonald's sack with used hamburger wrappers and empty fry containers out a car or pick-up window. The only way that mindset was going to be changed had to start with the younger generation—us. I can still remember seeing the old American Indian man on the hill looking down across the valley and seeing nothing but trash, and a single tear rolling down his face with the message, "People Start Pollution, People can stop it.""

"Yes, you're right, I do remember that ad and it did have an impact on littering and on me."

"Yeah, and the other educational message that I remember while growing up that was also geared toward children, was of preventing forest fires with Smokey the Bear. Jim, we can really make a difference with this book. What I envision is writing about Lucky and then at the end of the story, having a separate section or chapter that stands alone telling of the conditions and putting in some educational tips and factors into the book, geared towards both the older generation and younger generation. But the real change has to start at childhood because these children go home and tell their parents about what they have read or learned at school and a gradual change and mindset begins to occur."

"Rico, this is great stuff. I am thrilled and excited for this project and again, thank you and Connie for doing this and for both of your ideas."

(Author's note:) In 1971, a campaign was launched on Earth Day with the theme, "People Start Pollution. People can stop it." This campaign became known as the "Crying Indian ad," which featured actor Iron Eyes Cody. In the ad he portrayed a Native American man devastated to see the destruction and devastation of the Earth's natural beauty caused by the thoughtless litter and pollution of a modern society.

In 1975, Keep America Beautiful introduced its "Clean Community System" that encouraged local communities to prevent litter through education efforts, advertising, local research, mapping of litter "hotspots", and cleanup activities. During the height of the campaign, it received over 2,000 letters a month from people wanting to join their local programs. The "Clean Community System" evolved into "Keep America Beautiful" with its then current network of roughly 580 local "Keep My Town Beautiful" organizations nationwide. By the end of the campaign, locals had succeeded in reducing litter by a whopping, unbelievable 88%.

These types of education campaigns work, as did the Smokey Bear (or Smokey the Bear) as an advertising mascot that was created to educate the public about the dangers of forest fires. An advertising campaign featuring Smokey was created in 1944 with the slogan, "Smokey Says– Care Will Prevent 9 out of 10 Forest Fires." Smokey Bear's later slogan, "Remember...Only YOU Can Prevent Forest Fires", was created in 1947 by The Advertising Council. In April 2001, the message was updated to, "Only You Can Prevent Wildfires." According to the Ad Council, Smokey Bear and his message are recognized by 95% of adults and 77% of children.

And guess what, nearly all those adults were children when they first saw the campaign that began in 1944, over 70 years ago!

Readers, let's ALL do our duty to spay and/or neuter our pets, and spread the word to the younger generations.

6. Rico's 21 Favorite Dog & Animal Quotes

"Happiness is a warm puppy." – Charles Schulz

"I'm suspicious of people who don't like dogs, but I trust a dog when it doesn't like a person." – Bill Murray

"I've discovered a Sea World attraction with much more room for the animals and it's free. It's called the ocean." – Ricky Gervais

"Dogs never bite me, just humans." – Marilyn Monroe

"No matter how little money and how few possessions you own, having a dog makes you rich." – Louis Sabin

"Money will buy you a pretty good dog, but it won't buy the wag of his tail."
– Josh Billings

"Dogs are not our whole life, but they make our lives whole." – Roger Caras

"Every dog must have his day." – Jonathan Swift

"There's just something about dogs that makes you feel good. You come home, they're thrilled to see you. They're good for the ego." – Janet Schnellman

"There is only one smartest dog in the world, and every boy has it." – Anonymous

"I wonder if other dogs think poodles are members of a weird religious cult."
– Rita Rudner

"Scratch a dog and you'll find a permanent job." – Franklin P. Jones

"The only creatures that are evolved enough to convey pure love are dogs and infants." – Johnny Depp

"What counts is not necessarily the size of the dog in the fight; it is the size of the fight of the dog." – Dwight D. Eisenhower

"Don't accept your dog's admiration as conclusive evidence that you're wonderful." – Ann Landers

"If you think dogs can't count, try putting three biscuits in your pocket and then only give him two of them." – Phil Pastoret

"The average dog is a nicer person than the average person." – Andy Rooney

"I've seen the look in dogs' eyes, a quick vanishing look of contempt, and I am convinced that basically dogs think humans are nuts." – John Steinbeck

"Let sleeping dogs lie." – Robert Walpole

"Some of my best leading men have been dogs and horses." – Elizabeth Taylor

"Only a dog and his boy can take a simple ten-minute walk to the store and turn it into an adventurous journey of an entire day." – Rico Austin

7 The Bridge at the end of the Rainbow

There is a bridge between Heaven and Earth, and [it] is called Rainbow Bridge. When an animal that has been especially close to someone here on Earth dies, that pet goes to Rainbow Bridge. There are meadows and hills for all of our special friends so they can run and play together. There is plenty of food and water and sunshine, and our friends are warm and comfortable.

All the animals who had been ill and that were old are restored to health and vigor; those who were hurt or maimed are made whole and strong again, just as we remember them in our dreams of days and times gone by.

The animals are happy and content, except for one small thing; they each miss someone very special, someone who [they] had to leave behind.

They all run and play together, but the day comes when one suddenly stops and looks into the distance. His bright eyes are intent; his eager body quivers. Suddenly he begins to run from the group, flying over the green grass, his legs carrying him faster and faster.

You have been spotted, and when you and your special friend finally meet, you cling together in joyous reunion, never to be parted again. A shower of kisses falls on your face; your hands again caress the beloved head, and you look once more into the trusting eyes of your pet, so long gone from your life but never absent from your heart.

Then you cross the Rainbow Bridge together....

—Author Unknown

Source: http://www.petloss.com/rainbowbridge.htm

About the Author: Mi Vida Loca

"I have eight simple sentences of which I live by that cover most of my philosophy for and of life; each written by a different author during a different time; all profound." – Rico Austin

"Do unto others as you would have others do unto you."
– (Matthew 7:12) Bible

"The harder I work, the luckier I get."
– Henry Ford

"In order to write about life, first you must live it."
– Ernest Hemingway

"Never, never, never give up."
– Winston Churchill

"All that is necessary for the triumph of evil is for good men to do nothing."
– Edmund Burke

"Every rose has its thorn."
– Poison with Bret Michaels

"You'll see the true reflection of me when the tequila bottle is empty."
– Rico Austin

"Screw me once, shame on you; screw me twice, shame on me."
–Unknown

Rico was born and raised in Southwestern Idaho. He is the oldest of five boys and grew up in an area that was ripe for several adventures with his four younger brothers and numerous cousins. Rico grew up near farmland that produced potatoes, hay, hops, grain and corn. There were several fruit orchards and vineyards in the Snake River Valley as well, due to the extraordinary fertile soil.

Rico Austin first began writing seriously as a seventh grader at age thirteen. He was elected as reporter for the Eager Beaver 4-H Club in Marsing, Idaho, and started submitting weekly articles to the local newspaper. Rico then was elected reporter for the local FFA chapter his freshman and sophomore year, continuing to expand his writing ability. As a freshman, Rico took third place in the Marsing High School essay contest titled, "American Beef Farmers."

A few years out of high school he moved to (the "big city") of Boise and enrolled at Boise State University as a student and walk-on football player. However, he could not escape the allure of traveling the world and began writing and storing his experiences in hopes of someday becoming a novelist and writer. He began reading every chance he had. From contemporary novels to classical literature, Rico's love of storytelling was uncontrollable. He appeared occasionally at Boise's former Comedy Club as a stand-up comedian, retelling his stories of growing up in a comedic fashion.

Rico earned an associate's degree in marketing and sales from BSU. After a few years of low-level management positions, Rico moved to Hawaii for a short time, surfed the waters of Kaua'i and enjoyed the outdoors. He then moved to back to Idaho. In 1991, Rico moved to the Phoenix/Scottsdale area and continued his education receiving a bachelor's of business administration in international business from Grand Canyon University, and was named the "Outstanding International Business Graduate of 1995." That same year he was also selected as "Mr. Future Business Executive" at the State Leadership Conference that included all universities in the state of Arizona.

The summer before graduating, Rico went to Vilnius, Lithuania, and taught English (ESL). During fall semester of his senior year at GCU, Rico attended Staffordshire University in England where he also started on the American football team for the Staffordshire Stallions. Rico finished his MBA in international management at Thunderbird School of Global Management with a focus on the Latin American region and the Spanish language. He did this while working full-time as a feature writer and freelance journalist at the T-Bird school paper, DAS TOR. Rico wrote a few of his articles with DAS TOR especially for the foreign students of Latin America. Rico also won the first and only writing essay at DAS TOR in March 1997. The essay asked contestants to propose ways for Thunderbird to be improved. Rico used his humor, knowledge of several countries that he had visited and innovation to secure the winning essay. One of his most serious assignments and pieces of journalism were reporting on the Winterim class 97, "US Foreign Economic Policy" in Washington DC including the opening of the 105th Congress and the Inauguration of the President of the United States Mr. Bill Clinton.

Former Vice President Dan Quayle served as an invited interim professor by the Thunderbird School President, Dr. Roy Herberger for two semesters, and Rico was fortunate enough to be one of sixteen students selected to attend his class.

*Special note, Rico received an A from the VP for the two-credit elective class. Was it because of Rico's performance on studies or VP Quayle was afraid of what Mr. Austin might write in the paper?

Hollywood has even had an encounter with Rico. Those who watched *Baywatch* with the beautiful Pamela Anderson and David Hasselhoff, might recall Rico Austin in a cameo appearance in the episode, "Night of the Dolphin" in 1997, where he played the role of a drug lord on a huge yacht with sexy chicks. He and his graduate classmates watched the aired episode in the "old clock tower hanger" in the TV lounge. He was invited back for another episode by casting director Susie Glickman, but declined due to a conflict with finals at Thunderbird. Rico chose education over stardom; when questioned why, he responded, "No one can ever take your education away. Everything else can come and go and, most likely will."

Rico also acted in a commercial for the local market in Boise, ID, as a construction worker in *This Old House*, sponsored by BMC West.

Rico is an avid fisherman and has traveled far and wide to cast his line into many waters, including streams, lakes, ponds, rivers, seas and oceans. He has worked for a few international companies as both a sales manager and a marketing manager. In his spare time he has worked as a land developer and was a licensed realtor in Arizona. Should you decide to visit Arizona, Rico would be more than happy to show you around his great state of Arizona through his children's book, *ARIZONA Is Where I Live.*

Rico is happily married to a graphic artist from Minnesota. They make their homes in the "Land of the Sun," Scottsdale, Arizona, and San Carlos, Sonora, Mexico. He and wife Connie enjoy snorkeling, hiking, hanging by their swimming pool, and traveling to the different beaches of Mexico while sipping on a cold cerveza or margarita blended with Rico's favorite TEQUILA.

Rico was selected for the May 19th, 2013 issue to represent Arizona on fellow author, Annette Synder's popular blog, Fifty Authors from Fifty States, which spotlights writing professionals across the fifty United States.[1] He was again chosen to represent his home state of Idaho on March 23, 2014. [2]

Rico was also chosen from among several hundred writers and bloggers to help compile a booklet with 13 other prominent authors. *How to Create Credibility as*

a Freelancer - 70 Tips from a Collection of Experts was published in December 2009.

Favorite movie: *Gone with the Wind*
Favorite comedies: *The Hangover,* and *The Wolf of Wall Street*
Rico's favorite books are:
John Steinbeck's *East of Eden*
Ernest Hemingway's *The Old Man and the Sea*
J.R. Tolkien's *The Hobbit*
David Stuart's *The Guaymas Chronicles*
Jack London's *Call of the Wild*
E.B. White's *Charlotte's Web*
Wilson Rawls' *Where the Red Fern Grows*

---

1 http://annettesnyder.blogspot.com/2013/05/arizona-i-know-about-grand-canyon.html
2 http://annettesnyder.blogspot.com/2014/03/rico-austins-private-idaho.html

Writing History

Rico's first novel, *MY BAD TEQUILA* was published on September 11, 2010. This bestseller was number one during its first three years of being published for a total of thirty-seven weeks under the Mexico Travel genre, Kindle version on Amazon.com. Its first sixteen reviews were all five-star reviews. It has remained in the top 100 of Amazon's Top Rated list among readers within the Mexico Travel genre since its debut in the fall of 2010.

His first children's book, *ARIZONA Is Where I Live* was published February 14, 2013. This was the same day as Arizona's 101st birthday.

Rico's autobiography/memoir of when and how he met Elvis Presley's son, *In the Shadow of ELVIS, Perils of a Ghostwriter*, was published April 26, 2013.

Son of the KING, an ELVIS Paradox Unveiled is Rico's fourth book and is a biography published in February, 2014.

Rico finished his fifth book, *Author, Artist & Anyone's Personal Marketing Guide to Financial Success with 11 Proven Promotions including Blogs and Social Media,* in March, 2015.

Rico completed his other fifth book (literally, his sixth), which is an extension or addition of his previous marketing guide, *Entrepreneur, Realtor & Anyone's Personal Marketing Guide to Financial Success with 10 Proven Promotions including Blogs and Social Media,* in June, 2015.

Lucky book number seven is Rico's work as a wordsmith: *Mexico Got Lucky*. It is a non-fiction, mystery dog story that captures the true, incredible kidnapping of Lucky, a poodle-mix and the heart of a Mexican community in the towns of San Carlos, Guaymas, Hermosillo, Obregón and Empalme in trying to get Lucky back home to his owner. He finished *Mexico Got Lucky* in the second half of 2015.

In May of 2014, Rico joined the drivers and racing crews of the NORRA Mexican 1000 to write a travel/race book to accompany a documentary film that will be screened and made about the Baja race. Rico was invited and chosen by the sponsors of the race and the documentary film maker to write of this adventure. It took three years to complete *BAJA LOCO, Four Racing Days and Tequila Nights on the NORRA Mexican 1000* and placed at the Arizona Literary Contest in 2017 sponsored by the Arizona Authors' Association.

Book number nine, *Baby Tender Love*, was co-written and published in 2018 with his wife Connie Austin and is about her life growing up in northern Minnesota on a 660-acre farm with dairy cows, beef cattle, sheep, two dogs, a horse and cats too numerous to name. This incredible story centers around a childhood Christmas present–Baby Tender Love—a doll that Connie yearned for when she was eleven years of age, but was disappointed when she did not get the gift that year of 1973. However, the next Christmas she unwrapped a gift and it was Baby Tender Love; unfortunately she had outgrown that stage in her life and now was more interested in boys and talking with her girlfriends. The doll was put away and discovered many years later. The story tells of the hardships, laughter and fun of growing up with many animals, and the tragedy of losing her father at her young age of fourteen, leaving her mother and twelve-year-old brother to take care of the farm and daily chores. Rico wrote the first chapter and the last chapter and Connie Austin wrote everything in between. What an incredible story which ends many years later in Arizona. This book too has won a literary writing award.

Next on the completed writing list, published in 2021 making it Rico's tenth published book is a self-help guide for teenage boys and girls raised by single parents or from broken homes. This book was a labor of love, in hopes that through reading the book, it will make positive and great differences in young adult lives. The book, *BOY To Successful MAN, a Roadmap for Teens & Young Adults* is co-written by Rico Austin PhD and Dr. Suave Powers and covers twenty-five different chapters of life lessons from "Accepting Responsibility" to "Common Sense", to "Education", to "Spirituality vs. Religion", to "Manners", to "How to Treat a Woman", to "Secrets", to "No Texting while Driving", to "Attitude and Gratitude", to "Bathroom Etiquette", to "Proverbs Remembered and Restored." Each chapter ends with a relating quote to the lesson with a prominent life-changing quote by many a famous, and not so famous, a person. If just one young person chooses right instead of wrong because of a sentence she or he has read in this book, the authors' efforts will have been rewarded. The ultimate goal of this book is to help mold *BOYS to successful MEN!* This book placed third at the Arizona Authors' Association Literary Contest, and Rico's short story, *DOG,* took first place in the Short Story genre and was nominated and submitted by the judging committee for the coveted, Pushcart Prize.[3] This is Rico's

---

3 The Pushcart Prize is an American literary prize published by the Pushcart Press that honors the best "poetry, short fiction, essays or literary whatnot" published in the small presses over the previous year.

second short fiction story which has been nominated for the Pushcart Prize.

Rico has authored seven different genres within his first ten books, doing the nearly impossible task of writing in a multitude of genres for books and short stories, all while winning multiple awards for these works.

And then, finally a return with a sequel: *MY BAD TEQUILA dos.* Rico is considering quite possibly turning it into a trilogy of which his fans are greatly anticipating.

CPSIA information can be obtained
at www.ICGtesting.com
Printed in the USA
LVHW081146130822
725831LV00014B/313